SIMPLE TRUTHS

YOU WON'T HEAR FROM MOST POLITICIANS

DOUG MATHESON

Bloomington, IN  Milton Keynes, UK

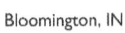

AuthorHouse™
1663 Liberty Drive,
Suite 200
Bloomington, IN 47403
www.authorhouse.com
Phone: 1-800-839-8640

AuthorHouse™ UK Ltd.
500 Avebury Boulevard
Central Milton
Keynes, MK9 2BE
www.authorhouse.co.uk
Phone: 08001974150

First published by AuthorHouse 12/15/2006

ISBN: 978-1-4259-7895-2 (sc)

Library of Congress Control Number: 2006910259

Printed in the United States of America
Bloomington, Indiana

DEDICATION

to Stephanie, Jonathan, Vanessa, and
all the children
who will inherit the nation, culture,
and world we leave them...
for better or for worse.

ACKNOWLEDGEMENTS

Time spent writing is preceded by time spent thinking and time spent reading. I thank my wife and children for their understanding of the moments I've been physically here but mentally elsewhere. And I thank the many outstanding, inquisitive, and demanding students who've kept me on my toes and made teaching even more worthwhile. You know who you are.

I would like to thank Lorraine Davis, Dennis Ingram, Lynne LeBlanc, Charlie McGonigle, and Lawerence Powers for reading early drafts and contributing their criticism, remarks, and suggestions.

I would like to thank my brother Murray Matheson for being my compatriot in the journey "where the evidence leads." Murray, it would have been an infinitely more lonely journey if not for our regular conversations and your being faithful to the evidence too.

My final thanks comes with a recommendation to my readers. A couple years ago I had a sense of hopelessness that enough Americans would come to see the long term over the immediate. Then in the spring of 2005 I found "The Opportunity", by Richard Haass. One quote was enough to renew my hope. He said, "America does not need the world's approval to act, but it does need the world's support to succeed." I cannot recommend this book too highly. Get it, read it.

A second book that has also been tremendously up-lifting in its combination of good sense, historic insight, and patient long-term view is "The Future of Freedom", by Fareed Zakaria. His distinctions between liberal and illiberal democracy, and his clear demonstration of prerequisites and limitations to democracy are truly insightful. Get this book too, and read it.

My faith in the average American continues to grow knowing that we have access to and are buying quality reading. To both these authors, thank you for keeping me optimistic. And while my writing is kept free of footnotes, I would like to specifically acknowledge here that the thoughts on the role of free markets, economic development, and stable democracies (p. 25 in The Role of Religion and p. 92 in Potpourri) are condensed from them.

Sincerely,

Doug Matheson

CONTENTS

PREFACE*

The enormity of the change in the security of our world since 9-11 doesn't need stressing; we virtually all sense it. On some days the primal fear brought by terrorism stares us in the face. On any and every day though, that vague, uncertain, insecurity is at least in the back of our minds. We want to fight and win. There is a difference though between fighting with intensity and winning skirmishes here and there while generating more long-term enemies vs. actually looking at our actions and attitudes from the long-term perspective, and finding a way to not only fight today's terrorists but to reduce their appeal and put tomorrow's terrorists in a steady decline.

That difference, between winning the moment's battle vs. focusing on the long-term war, is something I've become convinced not enough of us really think about. While we can't look forward to a near-future, specific day of victory in the war on terror, we can work toward minimizing it to the point where we will have restored a world with some basic assurance of security and normalcy.

The question is essentially whether or not we will let the war continue to broaden in terms of it involving nearly whole cultures and regions, or whether we can re-narrow the conflict to the extremist radicals who started it.

This is a critical difference at this juncture. Though we face a good number of other serious challenges, the potential for the highest quality of life ever known to man is on the immediate horizon. Modern science continues to improve our ability to produce food; we have made some progress on leveling out population growth; we continue to improve our understanding of the actual workings of the human genome and its application to health care; we have an increasingly widely accepted level of minimum standards of ethical treatment for all people and, in some circles, an improving level of tolerance and respect among religious communities; and the current limits to techniques used in detecting and eventually seeing extra-solar planets and other aspects of space exploration are constantly being pushed back. Indeed, we can have a long and bright future.

On the other hand, if we just fight and even win specific battles with terrorists, but don't narrow the conflict to the point of eventually being able to win the war with terror, the future, measured from a few years to multiple generations, could easily devolve into a modern repeat of the dark ages. This time around though, the crusades wouldn't kill just scattered thousands of involved volunteers. With weapons of mass destruction, modern crusades could not only kill millions, but could disrupt or destroy so many aspects of modern society and technology that we could be set back millenia... perhaps never again to arrive at our current potential.

It is critical then that we figure out how best to win the war with terror, not just the moment's battle. Winning this war is the urgent issue of this book, but the broad issue of this book is societal stability and progress. In today's world, a strong, stable, broad-minded, and foresightful leader on the international scene is necessary. America can be that leader. But in order to be externally strong and stable, and thus avoid an international power vacuum in which terrorism would thrive and humanity would suffer, we must put our internal house in order. In just 20 years we will hit the 250 year mark as a nation. Those 20 years will be eventful and significant, and assuming we can constructively weather them, we need to reflect on the longer run of making it another 250 years. It is that long view that will be the theme of the second half of this work.

Who am I to think I have something to add to the discussion of winning out over terrorism and maintaining a stable and sustainable society at home? Let me first say some of who I am not. I'm not an Ivy League graduate, I'm not a Washington insider, and I was not born to wealth or connections. I grew up a conservative

Christian, I went to graduate school at a regular state university, and I'm raising my family in small town America in a county that voted predominantly red. Like a good number of my fellow mid-Americans though, I'm finding my political voice and speaking up. Why I care particularly about international issues and have the guts to speak out from small town America has somewhat to do with my unusual but not unique background. I grew up in India as a missionary kid, went to high school in Singapore, and as an adult have lived and worked in Lebanon, Canada, and Rwanda. My experiences in Lebanon and Rwanda were particularly informative to my world view. However, the breadth of my life experience does not guarantee the correctness of what I assert any more than being born to privilege does; it is evidence and careful reasoning that should be used in evaluating anyone's assertions.

I have chosen to state the simple truths that follow in pretty direct words, thus you hold in your hands a compact book... it doesn't need to be long. Though I suspect that some may initially be offended, that is not my intent, and if they keep reading through the explanation and background to these truths, I think that many will get past feeling offended. My writing will not be interrupted with numerous citations; this is not a doctoral dissertation. My approach is rather to rely on common sense based on experience, a life-long habit of asking questions and actually listening to answers, reading, and thinking rationally. My intended target audience is my fellow mid-Americans… people who read and think, who don't blindly vote any party line, but who haven't really found their voice yet. We have too long let ourselves be polarized by extremists on either end of the political spectrum. The "squeaky wheel" radicals have dominated the discussion. It is time that we in the middle speak up and take responsibility for influencing policy. Even if you don't end up agreeing with me, end your silence. Participate in the public debate on how to strengthen our society and constructively interact with the dangerous world in which we find ourselves. Let's quit being silent followers of the supposed political elite… they can actually be pretty ignorant.

I'll state my first simple truth right here in the preface. If the war on terror is to be re-narrowed and eventually won, we must do more than fight existing terrorists. We must address what has made and apparently continues to make their cause attractive to so many. To the extent that we have had anything to do with creating the general conditions or specific situations which attract tomorrow's terrorist, (Simple Truth # 1.) **We bear significant responsibility for the growth of large-scale terrorism.**

Join the discussion.

TABLE OF CONTENTS IN DETAIL

(with simple truths under each respective chapter)

**SECTION I. THE IMMEDIATE & LONG-TERM
BATTLE WITH TERRORISM**

critical method... we should expect that it is going to take Muslims a while to broaden their willingness to critically analyze their own texts, beliefs, etc.

ST # 5:   America is a secular nation, not a Christian one.

(A word to Muslims)

CHAPTER 3. Reflections on Leadership

ST # 6:   The faith of a politician should be a side issue, as long as it isn't among his top self-descriptors... at that point it becomes a risk.

ST # 7:   Real confidence is based in knowing <u>how</u> best to continue to figure things out and wisely adjust to realities in life, not simply in knowing <u>what</u> you believe now and forever.

CHAPTER 4. Theater of the Absurd

ST # 8:   If our presence is perceived as unjustified by the Muslim world, as is the case with Iraq but wasn't with Afghanistan, we are probably serving to recruit more future terrorists than we are killing today. Is that a winning formula?

ST # 9:   We can't freely run around deposing dictators we don't like. In imposing our will around the world, what would that make us?

SECTION II. AMERICA'S DURABLE INTERNAL STABILITY

CHAPTER 5. Education

ST # 10: It not only takes effort on the part of teachers and schools, it takes effort and support beyond the school to ensure that kids get good educations and to raise performances.

ST # 11: Like life in general, in education you tend to get what you pay for.

ST # 12: Various aspects of "No Child Left Behind" and other federal mandates, including some involving "Highly Qualified" teachers, are unattainable or impractical goals.

ST # 13: The huge emphasis on pulling up the performance of our low and marginal students is taking time and effort away from talented and motivated students.

ST # 14: Anybody and everybody, however poorly educated the home background, can see the simple reality that putting effort into doing well in school opens up doors of opportunity in their future, and conversely, that dinging around and failing in school is going to result in unskilled and low-paying jobs.

CHAPTER 6. Science Education

ST # 15: The simplest and most direct explanation of the evidence of the fossil record, of comparative molecular biology (both DNA and amino acid sequences), of comparative anatomy, of geographic distribution, and of comparative embryology is evolution by natural selection.

ST # 16: Intelligent Design might be taught in a philosophy class, but it should not be taught in science because it short-cuts the key scientific process of seeking to understand natural mechanisms and it introduces articles of "faith" where "questioning" should be standard procedure.

CHAPTER 7. Potpourri (Immigration, Soft and Spoiled, Energy, & Affirmative Action)

ST # 17: The long-term economic and social health of our nation will be better off if we work to strictly limit immigration to legal immigration.

ST #18: The combination of exporting our jobs and importing our laborers while expecting to maintain our lifestyle is non-sustainable pie-in-the-sky. We must re-value hard work and re-evaluate our expectations.

ST # 19: Nuclear generated power is an essential part of our long-term energy viability, and the sooner, the more of it, the better.

ST # 20: Affirmative action has been a good thing, but its end should be in sight.

CHAPTER 8. A Balanced Budget

ST # 21: Having a higher tax rate, a progressive and substantially higher one, for the extremely wealthy isn't confiscatory or punitive… it simply has them pay disproportionately into supporting the free enterprise system from which they benefit disproportionately.

ST # 22: We have already made other adjustments that affect the average and poor… full SS benefits are available only at increasing ages, as it should be. If a system that was designed to look out for the broader good can make adjustments that affect the masses, surely it can make adjustments that affect the privileged.

ST # 23: The need for significant adjustments to reality in programs like Medicaid and Medicare is pressing too. In these cases it may be that we baby-boomers need to just suck it up and realize that not everything we wish for can be.

ST # 24: It is up to all of us the make sure that government is and does what is right.

SECTION I:

THE IMMEDIATE & LONG-TERM BATTLE WITH TERRORISM

CHAPTER 1.

THE BATTLE VS. THE WAR

SIMPLE TRUTH # 1. RESTATED:

We bear significant responsibility for the growth of large-scale terrorism.

After a fair number of the simple truths in this book, some of you may need patience to hear things out. If that's you, take a deep breath. This truth isn't about beating ourselves up like an abused wife finding ways to blame herself. It is simply about analyzing things to gain insight and ultimately end this crazy situation. First of all, we need to make a fine but significant distinction. I do NOT believe that terrorism is justified. We can though, seek to understand even wholly unjustified behavior. Studies of horrific crimes and child abuse regularly seek to understand the unjustified.

When various types of crazies arise, society doesn't necessarily need to introspect in search of reasons why. David Koresh (the Branch Davidian leader in Waco, Texas), Jim Jones (of Jonestown, Guyana), and Timothy McVay (of Oklahoma City) were crazy people who did terrible things, but we as a society did not need to soul-search for what was behind their craziness. Why not? Because they didn't succeed in getting multiple thousands of people to join them in a known conquest of violence against innocent civilians.

Osama bin Laden is crazy too. The trouble is, his craziness isn't nearly as easy to dismiss as simply that because his cause has attracted legions. Why has he attracted a large, committed, and self-sacrificing following that reaches far beyond the poor and disenfranchised? This is a question we must seek to answer.

A sports analogy might be useful before getting into the heart of the matter. As we know, in baseball they differentiate between earned and unearned runs. The difference between earned and unearned runs takes on added importance if you look at earned and unearned enemies. Some people are going to hate you and be your enemies even if you've done nothing to earn their hatred. They are your unearned enemies, and, in contrast to baseball, you have to accept that you'll have some. (And you better be ready to fight them and win.) On the other hand are your earned enemies, and you'd certainly be smart to figure out what you've been doing, probably unintentionally and unwittingly, to earn them. Then you can fix it, end up with a fraction of the enemies, and have a much better chance of winning the game.

So back to our question of what has made extremist/ radical Islam grow from a tiny fragment to what it is today.   Have we inadvertently been adding earned enemies to our unearned ones? Imagine for a moment that we all live in one big peculiar city that has its own form of order. Neighborhoods are ruled by organized and rather civil gangs. They don't exist to do trade in illicit drugs; they **are** the law enforcement agents, and to a great degree they cooperate across most neighborhoods. The leader of the main gang resembles Mike Tyson in his prime, and differences are settled in arranged bouts inside a regulation boxing ring. Now you and I happen to have some major beefs with the way this Tyson-like enforcer runs our lives. We can't get decent jobs, our kids don't get decent schooling, we can't leave, our wives live in fear, and we face constant humiliation. When we've brought up our grievances, the reply always includes references to settling our differences in the ring. Now you and I might be in good shape and decent athletes, but getting in the ring for a "fair fight" with Mike Tyson in his prime would be rather like committing suicide.

So when we stand no chance of winning a fair fight, what do we do? Well, we're going to resort to "unfair" techniques. True, if we have discerning character, we'll try to catch this enforcer himself in a dark alley with our baseball bats, and we'll leave the innocent members of his family alone.

As a young man working in Lebanon in 1980-81, I had occasion to witness war and peace, prosperity and poverty, hope and despair, and a depth of religious conviction (of several types) that made true believers willing to commit acts of violence. Before I left the middle-east, I took a little time to travel in Jordan and Israel. During all of this, I engaged anyone with whom I could communicate in conversation. I asked a lot of questions, and did a lot of listening.

Back in America a year later I called in to talk with a Larry King guest-expert on the middle-east. Among the things I said to them was something like, "The middle-east doesn't stand a chance for peace until and unless the Palestinian people have a legitimate and respected homeland." Both Larry and his guest concurred. Still a year after that, while teaching in a suburb of Los Angeles, I contacted representatives of both the Jewish and Palestinian communities to make presentations and lead discussion in my social studies class. Needless to say, it's a difficult issue.

I don't pretend for one second that the Palestinian homeland issue is the only thing that is behind al Queda's recruiting ability, but it has been a long-standing thorn in the side and is a significant contributing factor. The point for the moment is that we have been Israel's enforcer, we have given them largely unquestioning and one-sided support. The broad perception in the

Muslim/Arab world is that we are not even-handed in our handling of issues that affect them. (We all know that there are huge numbers of Muslims who are not Arab, and a fair number of Arabs who are not Muslim. I use the "/" symbol to mean "both" populations, not that they are the same.) Unable to step in the ring and win a fair fight with Israel and us, they resorted to unfair techniques. One can wish that they would have focused their unfair tactics on military targets (something that might actually have helped their cause), but they haven't. It doesn't make it right; it is dead wrong to attack innocent and uninvolved civilians. But it shouldn't be completely unbelievable that when you corner something in desperate circumstances, be they human or animal, they might react in violent desperation.

I will deal more with Israel and religion's role in the world's state of affairs in a later chapter, but for now let me reassure anyone inclined to think otherwise… I believe Israel has a right to exist. The world's support in the creation of Israel in the aftermath of the holocaust was justified. But some aspects of that creation lead to wronging another people, and two wrongs don't make a right.

The real issue here and now is that we have to do more than fight today's terrorist. We have to figure out what drives their recruiting of tomorrow's terrorist, and we have to have the guts to begin to do something about it. In order to fully reveal Osama bin Laden's craziness for what it is, we have to deprive him of the few legitimate issues he mixes in with his irrational agenda. There really are millions of civil, right thinking Muslims/Arabs. We want to help isolate al Queda as the extremists they are; instead our recent foreign policy has ended up isolating us.

It is at times easy for us in the west to wonder where the civil, right thinking Muslims are. The TV images we see naturally don't focus on them, and unless you've lived among them, assuming that moderates almost don't exist can creep into our thinking. It is simply an exaggerated case of the same general phenomenon we suffer here. Those in the middle, the majority, get drowned out by the hard-liners. The challenge there, as here, is to have the middle step up and speak up. Let us not lose focus though, by being side-tracked to what we expect them to do. That's a challenge they must deal with, and one I address directly at the end of the next chapter. We must stay focused right now on what we have been doing, are doing, and can do.

The Palestinian issue is an old recruiting tool, and our invasion of Iraq is a new one. After 9-11, the world at large, including significant portions of the Muslim/Arab world, was with us. We had broad and even overwhelming support in going into Afghanistan to oust the Taliban and get al Queda. At that point moderate Muslims (the majority), despite the long-standing Palestinian issue and perhaps other lesser issues, weren't attracted to al Queda. As we began to rattle our sword over Iraq, that began to change. If our own allies were distancing themselves from us, what do you think your average Arab/Muslim (who while not hating us, did hold us in mistrust and suspicion) was doing? When we could have continued to build our team and isolate al Queda, our obvious plans to invade Iraq (premised on reasons even our allies doubted) actually ended up isolating ourselves and building al Queda's team.

Am I saying Saddam was a good guy? No Way! But was our leadership taking the time and using insight to see the long run? Equally, No Way! The really sad thing is that there were people within ear-shot of the president who were warning him of this folly, but he had very selective hearing. There is a critical difference between truly imminent threat and a regime we happen to intensely dislike and mistrust.

Another very sad thing about our invasion of Iraq and the predictable (and predicted) difficulties it has brought is that we, the American population, 'passed' on a chance to show the world, and moderate Muslims in particular, that we didn't agree with the invasion. When someone demonstrates their closemindedness and lack of foreign policy insight and foresight on the job, it is sad when we let fear (of unknown leadership and of then fresh al Queda threats) keep us from sending the world a worth-while message. In the 2004 election our votes could have said, "We were wrong to let this man take us there." The ever-increasing number of mid-Americans who wish they had said that then, have said it now. We, the people, just have begun to seriously correct a major al Queda recruiting tool. Never mind the Downing Street memo on one hand, and never mind the conclusions of the 9-11 commission on the other hand. There are memoirs yet to be written which may well continue to reveal a president obsessed early-on with Iraq, and just looking for the right excuse. While talking about the dangers of Iraq and weapons of mass destruction and then acting on it, Mr. Bush succeeded in enlarging al Queda's recruiting base, thus making it not less but more likely that one day we may well face the horrors of a nuclear flash over civilians.

It is an interesting side-light to our fight with terrorism to note how our invasion of Iraq has also affected our relations with established regimes like Iran. We must keep the broad context in mind. For at least a decade prior to our invasion of Iraq the relatively "secular" middle in Iran was growing in numbers and influence, and the hard-liners were being weakened. When we invaded Afghanistan with the overwhelming support of the world at large, most in Iran didn't object even though the shared border and close American presence probably stirred some hard-liners.

Then we planned and executed our invasion of Iraq. Now our presence in Afghanistan and Iraq, and our influence in Pakistan nearly surrounds Iran. It is no-doubt far too easy for us to say something like, "So what? We're the good guys. What do they have to worry about?" But if you are a hard-liner in Iran, you now have more evidence to support your talk of America's material imperialism, injustice, or whatever fear-mongering theme you choose. And if you were one of the once growing moderates in Iran, you are likely driven either toward radical positions or into silence.

In the tough situation we find ourselves in with regard to how to handle Iran, we can only wish we still had the global political capital we had after 9-11 but before invading Iraq. If we had that capital, not only would we be in a much stronger position to deal with them, but **more significantly, we quite likely wouldn't be in a confrontational situation at all because the radicals wouldn't even be in power there**. We, by poorly thought through strategic decisions, drove them back from growing moderate influence into the arms of waiting radicals. It really shouldn't surprise us when our surrounding an independent state with our military power results in them becoming more confrontational and less cooperative.

The discussion of whether or not President Bush out-right lied to us in making the case for invading Iraq seems almost too hot for objective discussion. I have sometimes thought that the overall evidence doesn't point to deliberate, planned deception. Rather, we elected a man who has shown no natural tendency to introspection on his own motives and no habit of careful analysis of possible realities beyond what he happens to believe. To compound matters, he has never tried to correct for what he doesn't see as a weak spot. He proudly proclaims that he believes *what* he believes; but he appears to have never thought of and certainly hasn't proclaimed *how* he figures things out. To one degree or another we all share the tendency to reach the conclusions we want before we fully digest the evidence. Then we stick with those conclusions, political or religious, for the rest of our lives. The more we can be aware of and fight that temptation, the more reliable both our thought processes and our conclusions.

The difference between decisions, personal or national, made based on what we *want* to believe (our ideology) versus those based on objective analysis of evidence is of vital importance. The single greatest area of importance bears directly on whether we manage to narrow the current conflict or let it mushroom out of control.

Various congregations have invited speakers whose message seems to be "All Muslims have the goal of taking over the world for Allah." Under attack as we are, some seem to want to believe that; they sit and nod their heads while receiving a message from someone who claims to have insight, telling them what they already believe.

Think about this for a second. Here we are in a society where the least educated among us in general have graduated from high school. They have had at least one class in world history, in logical thinking through geometry, in the scientific method and valid conclusions, and in at least rudimentary aspects of literary analysis (recognizing bias, etc.). The more educated among us have had even more opportunity to see the world broadly and objectively. **If we, a relatively well educated culture, are still inclined to listen to extremists among us who beat drums of fear, who broadly portray the whole Muslim culture as evil and violent, what in the world do we expect of them?**

Hands down, despite good numbers of them being well educated, the masses there have not had as much opportunity for basic education. They have their own fundamentalists beating the drums of fear and hatred. **Are they somehow going to be less susceptible to believing ideologically driven nonsense about us?**

If we don't step up to the plate and rationally and calmly confront our own ideologues (be they top politicians, fellow church members, or co-workers) who simply spout what they happen to believe, we will be guilty of having let the conflict unnecessarily and tragically broaden. We **must** meet this challenge. We can re-narrow the conflict.

If you still find yourself tempted to follow leaders "of strong conviction," who really believe what they believe, allow me to point out that the ultimate in leaders with a depth of faith and conviction is Osama bin Laden. He never pauses in self-analysis or reflection of what beyond his belief system might make good sense. He doesn't subject his preferred beliefs to the possible modifications that objectively verifiable evidence might bring. He sticks to his guns. Is that the kind of leadership we want to follow… is that how we ourselves want to sort out life? If we can't resist the temptation to give our chosen beliefs priority over objectively verifiable evidence, we're in for a world of hurt because this conflict will broaden, deepen, and intensify.

The flip-side to being firmly set in our preferred beliefs without regard for real verifiable evidence is very liberating and allows us to avoid unnecessary conflict… and will be further discussed in the next chapter.

Several weeks before we invaded Iraq I listened in as some of my students discussed the apparently up-coming invasion. Seeing me listening and knowing that I had a tendency to see things from a different perspective, a couple of these young rural republicans-in-the-making challenged me to join in and say something. I gave them this illustration: Imagine our school has a total stud athlete. He's bigger, stronger, faster, and has great coordination and vision; he is by far the best athlete our school has ever had. Now imagine that one of the rival schools in our league has the same kind of stud. They're alike except for attitude. One of them swaggers down the hall. On the field or court his approach is "just gimmie the ball." The other guy walks with humility that almost hides his strength. On the field or court he loves the "assist." Yes, you can count on him at crunch time if you need him, but he loves sharing the load and the glory with his teammates. Now, which guy is more likely to develop enemies? And which guy's teammates are more likely to stick with him should he really need them? With a nod, most of my students acknowledged that they got it. We have allies, teammates. We can leave them feeling like their input doesn't matter, or we can be a genuine team player. My students also saw that our attitude, perceived even if not always real, of swaggering around the globe doing it our way, no matter what, only makes more people pass the critical balance point from mistrusting us to hating us. We lend our real enemies a stronger recruiting base and make it more likely we'll meet with more proverbial baseball bats in dark allies.

What now? It's extremely tough. I know I'll disappoint some in this, but I am not in favor of withdrawing the troops now, or at any artificially imposed date. To quit while chaos reigns in Iraq would only embolden today's terrorists and add the momentum of a win to their future recruiting. I don't think George Bush would have the honesty and courage to personally step up and say, "I was wrong to push for this war, but I'm not going to commit a second wrong to try to make a right. We can't leave prematurely. We must stay until we've helped the Iraqi people get their feet on solid ground." (Although limited admissions of errors like prisoner abuse, civilian casualties, inflammatory talk, and underestimating the power of instant information are small steps in the right direction, they don't get close to "I was wrong to push for this war.") I believe it would be helpful though if someone reasonably high in the State Department articulated something along those lines because it would actually help wrap things up. We'd be less "suspect" of having ulterior motives.

Is it possible that things will continue to get worse over there? Unfortunately, yes. Could we reach a point reminiscent of the last helicopters lifting off the embassy roof in Saigon? Again, yes. We must though, have the guts, courage, and willingness to sacrifice to make every effort to ensure that doesn't happen. How will we know if we reach the point of truly having lost? I don't know, and fervently hope we never find out. If that ever happens, during the decades in which terrorism will be worse, rather than simply pointing fingers back at Bush, Cheney, Rove, and Rumsfeld, I hope we have the honesty and guts to accept our own role in the whole mess. We, regular citizens across America, passively let our country be lead by short-sighted leaders who lacked insight into the complexity of other cultures and our real and perceived role in the world; we let our beliefs out-weigh rational analysis of actual evidence… we let the conflict broaden. This isn't about assigning "blame," it is simply about learning from experience. The real lesson may be that we all have to speak up and do whatever it takes to get the ear of our leaders. Even if we ultimately succeed in getting Iraq to stability and avoiding the surge of terrorism that losing would bring, the same lesson is there.

No-doubt there are some who immediately write off talk of fixing what we've done or are doing that contributes to terrorism's growth as simply naïve. Well, let's remind ourselves of what naivite involves. It is being unaware of basic realities that should be known at certain developmental levels. Thus the "hawk" thinks that it is naïve to analyze and fix our role in terror's existence and growth because he supposes that it ignores the basic reality that there are genuine bad-guy crazies who must be fought. Note though, that he is himself being naïve because he is ignoring the basic reality that you actually can broaden your enemy's long-term appeal by broadening the conflict to include whole cultures and religions, and by being go-it-alone… my way or the high way.

Remember the baseball analogy? We have got to get better at fighting our unearned enemies while not gathering new earned enemies. If we can succeed at limiting ourselves to unearned enemies, at re-narrowing the conflict, we will indeed stand a much better chance of winning this war.

CHAPTER 2.
THE ROLE OF RELIGION

If times were normal, I wouldn't be speaking out on our role in terrorism and I certainly wouldn't be saying anything about anyone's religious beliefs. But these are not normal times. The potential for large-scale disaster if we let ourselves fall into a modern version of the crusades-of-old is simply too great. It is not an accident that I refer to the historical crusades. Those were cultural wars, ostensibly fought for religious reasons. Kings and Sultans invoked the name of God, then generals marshaled their volunteers in the name of God, and on both sides those volunteers died for their beliefs in their God.

Today we have religious fundamentalists of the Islamic variety behind terrorism. They invoke the name of God and are willing to die. Amazingly, many in our educated modern country respond as if they think that the best response to religious extremism is to develop and strengthen our own brand of religious extremism. Both citizens and political leaders, soldiers and pastors can be heard invoking the name of God in our battle with terrorists. Can we think for a moment that declaring God to be on our side makes it so? In actuality, mimicking them and declaring God to be on 'our' side may simply give our enemies more motivation to prove us dead wrong.

I go into a number of simple truths related to religion with great reluctance. I think of religious belief as near and dear to the heart, and your choice of religious belief doesn't have to answer to my rationale. But in America today there is a serious effort to force the Evangelical Christian view into public policy… into domestic law via the legislature and the courts, and even into foreign policy via the administrative branch. Because this impacts the scale of the battle, drawing in whole cultures and countries instead of leaving fundamentalists isolated, I cannot withhold comment.

I know in this area that some will inevitably be offended. If you happen to be a "true believer" of some type, I hope your idea of God includes forgiveness and patience, because you may find that you need both to get through some of this. If you persevere, I think some of you will be persuaded by the evidence and good sense I offer. True die-hards will never be convinced, and that's ok. It is my hope though that I do convince here-to-fore too silent mid-Americans that we cannot afford to stay silent and let ourselves be dragged into a religion-dominated society and religiously driven wars.

SIMPLE TRUTHS

2. Muslim fundamentalists are a serious impediment to peace.

Duh! No real discussion needed here. But in case some of the non-extremist Muslims of the world wind up reading this, it is you more than anyone else who can effectively isolate your extremists and clear your own good name. For your community's sake, and for the sake of the future of mankind, step up and work to isolate extremists. More on this theme later.

3. Jewish fundamentalists are a serious impediment to peace.

Not so obvious to some, this may merit some discussion. There are secular Jews around the world. I've met and had discussions with some in Israel and in America. It is my distinct impression that they have reasonable expectations, a willingness to compromise with Palestinians, and a desire to live and let live in peace.

There are also fundamentalist Jews around the world. I've also met and had discussions with some. They've been honest in expressing their clear vision of the world. They are Jews, God's chosen people, the apple of his eye. The rest of us are Gentiles… to be tolerated at best. It's not our fault, it's just how it is.

Their claims, to special status and to land are relatively easy for most any of us to shrug off as nonsense or rationalize as "conditional." But if your historical land is the same piece as theirs, as is the case with the Palestinians, shrugging is not so easy. For a couple generations now you have had to deal with settlements and fundamentalist settlers occupying progressively greater portions of what had been yours. If secular, moderate, Jews had been in firm control of their politics, they would have been able to implement policies which the Palestinian people, the majority of whom are not radicals, would have found acceptable.

4. Christian fundamentalists are a serious impediment to peace.

Now wait a minute some may say. This is not so easy, and so may require significant discussion. Along the way we will note a number of sub-set simple truths.

An increase in prayer, both public and private, was a very understandable reaction to 9-11. On that day we came under attack, and wherever we were, we felt that visceral fear; indeed, there are almost "No atheists in fox-holes." But various religious and political leaders have used that initial primal fear and the subsequent lasting feeling of insecurity to magnify our cultural differences. Rather than think analytically, to look objectively at evidence history can offer us, too many leaders have sought followers who are blindly willing to simply strengthen their belief systems. Too many have been willing to embrace the idea that "God" is on any side in a war, and since He must be on our side, all of the believers in other, "false", religions must be wrong and must be fought as a whole group.

The Arab/Muslim world reads our columnists and hears rhetoric coming out of our churches and from various of our far-right elected politicians. Those hearing and reading these comments are not unaffected. When they see that they have been painted with a very broad brush, their reaction is naturally to assume that the radical statements reflect our majority opinion, thus painting us with a very broad brush. And so the cycle goes. Fairly quickly you can go from narrow, albeit strong, ideological differences to broad cultural conflict, to having whole countries a lot closer to all-out war. How quickly this happens depends to a great degree on the relative degree of education vs. primitiveness of the countries in question.

This brings us to a number of subset simple truths.

#4a. The more primitive the society, the less likely they are to question their own basic religious beliefs.

#4b. The more educated the society, the more they should be able to acknowledge that different religious views are equally legitimate, and that religion isn't subject to verification of objective facts.

I've listened more than once to good Christians comment on the primitiveness of cultures and societies where voters base their decisions on the clan, ethnic group, or religious affiliation of the candidates. It's ironic then when those same Christians state their position on a political race or issue here in America with words like, "Because he/she is a born again Christian," or, "That's the Christian position."

#4c. It took Christianity multiple centuries to reach the point of going through the renaissance and developing the historical-critical method... we should expect it is going to take Muslims a while to broaden their willingness to critically analyze their own texts, beliefs, etc.

This puts the onus on us to be more patient with them than we can expect them to be with us. I must stress though, I'm not talking of patience with terrorism. We must fight that, not only with strength, but with wisdom. Rather, I'm pointing to patience with little irritations like their narrow definition of truth and them calling us infidels. That doesn't need to hurt us, and we certainly don't need to retort with similar name-calling.

I know some who still genuinely feel that they are not being paranoid in fearing that Muslims as a whole are out to get us, to conquer the world. I would simply point out that while radical fundamentalist Muslims indeed are, radical fundamentalists of any kind have never shown an ability to stay unified. Shoot, look at your own Christian denomination or even local congregation. The more inflexibly convicted and assertive any subgroup, the more likely they are to fracture from within. We don't have to fear a unified Muslim attack… unless it is we who unify them with our own irrational attacks. Fundamentalists can't keep a united front… or even a united core.

In any case, the best long-term way to prevent a global take-over by any fundamentalist group is through promoting real education and broad economic engagement. Real education, not indoctrination, promotes independent and analytical thinking… the very antidote to fundamentalism. And economic engagement that involves infinitely more than exploiting mineral wealth promotes the development of a real middle class. Both of these are really prerequisites to lasting democracy; trying to do democracy first isn't likely to work for a multitude of reasons.

Back to the immediate need for our calm patience with the broad Muslim culture. While narrowly and intensely fighting terrorism, it is worthwhile remembering that the answer to them declaring their very nationhood and form of governance to be based on one religion doesn't need to be that we declare ourselves to be a nation based on another religion.

5. America is a secular nation, not a Christian one.

This is a hot button, and if it weren't for the definite movement trying to impose the opposite I wouldn't touch it; but we mid-Americans must stand up or get railroaded.

Some relatively recent events and trends can help make this discussion less dry and abstract and become much more real and practical. Remember "Justice Sunday?" That huge televised meeting in Louisville seemed intended to galvanize the true-believer Christians among us into supporting various aspects of making our Christian values into the law of the land. That meeting got a lot of attention.

At almost the same time several pastors in my hometown held a "Celebration of All Faiths." A half-dozen people attended. Surprising? No, but why not? Why indeed would two meetings, both on religious themes and both organized by religious people, draw such different levels of interest? The leaders of the first meeting focused on points that divide us, while the leaders of the second meeting focused on issues that unite us. But should it begin to raise our concerns when unity draws a yawn but divisiveness draws a crowd? I trust the answer is obvious. The point for the moment is that if we don't carefully watch ourselves, we are easy prey to divisive issues and divisive people. If we let ourselves and our fellow-citizens be herded down such artificially imposed divergent roads, our country is in for an unfortunate, unnecessary, and destructive battle.

Let me share a list of reasons for not imposing our particular faiths into politics and the laws of our land. Before I get into the details, let me reassure those of you who identify yourselves as evangelical Christians. Your faith has as much legitimacy as anybody's, and even your desire to share your faith isn't a problem. The problem arises when you try to impose your belief system on others.

HERE'S THE LIST:

1. You wouldn't want others to impose their religious beliefs on you, so don't do it to them. (Remember, "Do unto others…")

2. Respect for freedom of speech, religion, etc. is a fundamental ideal in the Constitution.

3. **Religion at the level of the individual's heart can solve problems, but religion at the level of public policy or law creates problems.** Just check what the Taliban accomplished. (If you're tempted to say "Yeah, but they had the wrong religion," there are Christian examples.)

4. Having the humility to accept others' religious faiths as being just as legitimate as yours, and just as likely to be right, is a very constructive step toward peace. (Remember, humility is a Christian virtue.)

5. Recognizing that among the many reasons you are a Bible-believing Christian is the coincidence that you were born into it, and that religious beliefs themselves are things of the heart and therefore impossible to objectively verify can help you relax and not feel driven to convince or coerce others.

6. Remember Christ's attitude and approach. He set out to positively affect the quality of individual's lives by affecting their hearts and minds, not by trying to change the laws of the land.

Lest the Christians among us feel too picked-on, let me clearly state that to impose anti-religion is as wrong as imposing a particular religion. I don't live around many Jews or Muslims, but if I did I wouldn't have any trouble responding in a friendly and gracious way to "Happy Hanukkah" or "Happy Ramadan." To have trouble accepting a wish for a Merry Christmas is ridiculous, and a Christmas Tree, even on government property, is hardly a religious endorsement. That blends invisibly into "culture," as where a nativity scene may well be on that slippery slope we're better off avoiding. Who needs it on government property when we have all the freedom in the world to put it on our church or private property?

As we started out noting though, just as anti-religion can get carried to ridiculous extremes, the religious right can get carried away too. When the most important qualification for an appointed judge is that "_____ is a person of faith," when the new right knows best how to teach "science," when big government is the enemy until it is enforcing their values, then we know we've got some things badly out of whack. To those who might still insist on thumping your Bibles into others' lives, at least preface your comments with something like, "In my view of God…" And don't even try the "It's not my view, it's the Biblical view," approach. Firstly, pick the right text and even slavery and racism are Biblical. Secondly, it is arrogant to proclaim that the Bible is the only right view of God.

In a nutshell, if we can begin to relax and be less defensive about our beliefs, we can be as serious as we want about our own faiths, but accepting of others'. Despite our greatest worries, we're not going to fall apart as a nation because we're not following one particular view of "God's way;" however, we might fall apart because we quit respecting each others' values and religious freedom, including the conviction that there may be no god. For those who insist that America is a Christian Nation, imagine this: The founding fathers are faced with a choice. They can, A. form a government where faith (even our Christian faith) dictates the laws of the land, or B. establish a government which respects faiths of all kinds, and ensures that laws are based on our Constitution. You don't have to imagine it. They chose B. Some may not like the term "Secular," but that is exactly what our government was designed to be.

Critics of the secular nation ideas expressed here take multiple angles. One of these is to point to the demographics of our founding fathers in particular and of the early colonies in general, and to equate our obvious majority Christian "heritage" with "form of government." This mistaken equating of majority statistics with form of government isn't the end of trouble with semantics. Some have real trouble with the word "secular." They seem to feel secular means evil at worst, or devoid of any values at best. Without resorting to dictionary definitions, I would simply suggest that the laws of a secular nation are based on "common ground" between religious groups of all sorts and non-religious groups, and on "common sense." The "common ground" part necessarily involves not letting any single group, even a Christian majority, establish totalitarian or theocratic rule.

Another argument with the secular nation idea focuses on the fundamental idea of religious "truth." They insist that the Jesus of the Bible is the only way. They reject the idea that religious faiths of all kinds involve leaps of "faith", and they try to convince themselves and others that religious truth is based on evidence and that they have the objective truth. It is not my goal to disprove anyone's faith; indeed no faith can be disproven any more than it can be proven. Still, I will point to some realities that lend support to my assertion that faith needs to be held in humility (items 4 and 5 on my list) to be constructive. One of those realities is that many within Christianity like selected facts found in archaeology from recent millennia, but never bother to really explore the deeper times, evidence, or issues of paleontology, molecular biology, astronomy, or the details of other faiths. That's okay. Most don't explore so comprehensively; but they shouldn't assume that the reality they've bothered to become aware of is anything near actual full-scale reality.

I do not mean to discount the deeply personal "evidence" that some feel they must consider. I simply think that they would do well to recognize that others have different personal evidence, and that none of it is objectively verifiable.

In fighting against the secular nation idea some resort to quoting famous patriots or Supreme Court Justices whose opinions were that we are a Christian nation. Patrick Henry is sometimes held up as an advocate of the Christian nation, but I for one can't believe he was so narrow-minded and short-sighted as to offer to die for only his particular flavor of liberty. As to the Supreme Court, it is ironic that the same people who decry it for failure and faulty logic in cases where they don't like the decision, quote it as an authority beyond question when it concluded that we are a Christian nation. The troublesome reality is that we as citizens have the responsibility of "reviewing" the opinions rendered by the court, and of recognizing when it speaks from its historical context more than from any objective truth. Remember, even the Supreme Court upheld slavery.

Some express the concern that if we don't have God, the Ten Commandments, and the prospect of hell, our society will fall apart at the seams because nobody will have a reason to behave. Well, it makes one wonder why we have laws on the books, and punishments to go with them, intended to give structure and stability to our society. More to the point though, the people who feel that fear of punishment from God is the central stabilizing factor in society have pretty low levels of moral development. Without getting too lost in the details, many may vaguely remember from something like psychology 101 that Lawrence Kohlberg did some interesting research which showed a progression of moral development.

KOHLBERG'S THREE BROAD LEVELS WERE:

1. PRE-CONVENTIONAL. Here, as is typical in young children, decisions of right or wrong are made on punishment vs. reward, and on the perceived power of the rule-maker.

2. CONVENTIONAL. Here decisions of right or wrong are made based on respect for the expectations of the family, group, or nation. It involves conforming to social conventions.

3. POST–CONVENTIONAL. Here decisions of right or wrong are made autonomously based on principles that have validity beyond group borders and without consideration of enforcement or consequence.

Interestingly, many people do not mature beyond level 1. But that should not be used as an excuse to keep some particular religion and God central in society. There may be various good reasons to keep a personal belief in God, but religion's role in controlling societal behavior becomes pretty shallow thinking. There are other effective motivations for good behavior. I want my kids to be able to say "Dad was a good, if far from perfect, man," and I want to feel that I will leave the world a better place than I found it.

Some complain that secularists are trying to completely exclude Christian influence from government. Though I suspect there are extremist secularists out there (witness the whole Merry Christmas/Christmas-Tree spat) whose agenda may include complete exclusion, I think that most who assert that we are a secular nation are simply seeking to ensure that no faith be allowed to dominate our government as some in the neo-conservative movement seem to want. I think most any of us would have a hard time finding a better starting point for the laws of the land than "Treat others like you would like to be treated."

In wrapping up this section on the role of religion in our society, and therefore in our conflicts with other societies, I guess the simplest summary is to say "Let's keep some humility in our faiths, and let's not impose any of our faiths into government policy, domestic or foreign." Let's recognize that despite some of our fondest wishes, religion is extra-rational. Many people in many religions don't have too much trouble with that, but to the more fundamentalist Christians among us, I offer you this challenge: Set up a jury of peers from around the world, an educated person from every faith you can think of, including your precise brand of Christianity. Now let them try to convince one another with their objectively verifiable "facts." You know as well as I do how far they would or wouldn't get.

Yes, the founding fathers went out of their way to ensure that our government would respect faiths of all kinds, yet establish none. If you are offended by the term secular, find another one to describe it. The bottom line is that religious freedom, and every other freedom implies respect for, and a degree of understanding and acceptance of our differences. None of that leads to imposed values. Don't resent it, celebrate it; it could be somebody else imposing their values on you.

True die-hards will never be convinced, and I can live with that; it's the majority of my fellow mid-Americans who think issues through whom I hope I've given some food for thought. Why do I write, why do I risk the anger of some, why do I care? Because in this day and age, when we as a nation and culture are under attack from extremist terrorists, it is all too easy for us to succumb to our fears and lack of understanding and to lash out reflexively, thus widening a conflict that could be narrowed. Whether we like it or not, the world is increasingly a global village. We can fill the role of constructive leader, who not only seeks our own security, but the general good of all. Conversely, we can be as primitive and divisive as our current enemies in being dead sure that our particular belief system is exactly right and everyone should just fall in line. In case a borderline die-hard will consider a little gem of wisdom from a long-time conservative, I would suggest reading George F. Will's "Last Word" article in the May 23, 2005 Newsweek. His closing paragraph states, "America is currently awash in an unpleasant surplus of clanging, clashing, certitudes. That is why there is a rhetorical bitterness absurdly disproportionate to our real differences. It has been well said that the spirit of liberty is the spirit of not being too sure that you are right…"

A PERSONAL POST-SCRIPT TO CHRISTIANS

I genuinely hope that, after reading the whole, those who were irate after reading the previous rather direct simple truths have found room to relax. I'm not attacking Christians; nearly everyone near and dear to me is a conservative Christian, and I wouldn't attack them. I'm not saying Christian beliefs are "wrong." Rather, I'm simply saying that since there is no way of objectively proving that they're "right," it is best, wisest, and most contributing to broad peace among man to hold our beliefs with humility. I know some who, for deep reasons of their own, can't stand the thought that their beliefs systems may not be "right," and I am sorry if I've shaken your sense of security.

A WORD TO MUSLIMS

If you are a Muslim and have read the preceding pages, you are most probably a moderate and deserving of respect because you read broadly, risking exposure to ideas which may be different than yours. You think things through for yourself. Being a moderate who reads a variety of sources, you would know that I am not alone in America or the west in calling on our fellow-moderates to step up and confront our radicals. You would know that we moderates recognize our national mistakes and are taking steps to correct them. We moderates, Christian and secular, can best limit our radicals here... we are on the inside. And you should know that you, Muslim moderates, can best limit the growth and affects of your radicals within Islam... you are on the inside.

This is no trivial side point. It is deadly serious. Unfortunately for you, your radicals advocate extremes of violence that I don't believe you can find in any branch of any other religion. Your challenge is indeed a big one... but you must step up to it. We outsiders to Islam can't get the attention of your radicals, we often don't know precisely who they are, and they won't listen to our logic anyway.

Your radicals won't be easily inclined to listen to your logic either, but you at least have a beginning point. You must recognize and outspokenly condemn the wrong aspects of radical Islam. It is not just the west that you would be helping in wrestling control away from your radicals… you will be helping yourselves, and all of humanity.

You have to know that if your radicals continue to gain influence, we in the west won't continue to act in as limited a fashion in our opposition to radical Islam's growth. If you don't step up, you will have proven that our radicals, who believe virtually all of Islam is violent, were right. And you will have given them the necessary excuse some of them are looking for to justify all-out broad cultural war. It is the hope of avoiding that exact scenario that drives me to write this book.

To make the challenge you face concrete and specific, let me mention a number of steps which I trust you will ultimately agree are reasonable. **You need to recognize that religious freedom is a good thing, and speak out and take action in its favor.** If you don't want Hindus or Christians forcing their religion on you, surely you can embrace the general idea that religious freedom is good for all. The practice of not even allowing your own people to choose their religion while actively exporting Islam with the sword (or bomb) simply does not recognize religious freedom, and you need to begin to change that.

You need to confront Imams and others who advocate the spread of Islam by violent means. You need to proclaim with words and actions that Israel has a right to exist without constant threat. You need to oppose your radicals who seek to control all aspects of societal behavior by one set of religious laws. It is ridiculous that an Islamic community within a sovereign nation would demand to be able to impose Islamic law in any part of that country.

As a simple practical matter, you can't imagine that the west will passively watch as you let violence come out from among you or as you progressively exercise forced control over communities in our countries. You must know that we can't judge your attitudes, behavior, and motives based on how well you behave when you are a small minority. Rather, we must look to places where you are either a large minority or a majority. Based on that we can reasonably determine if it is in fact safe and wise to continue to grant you the same freedoms we grant to all other religions. If you reveal yourself to be a cancer which grows quietly until it takes over with a vengeance, you will find yourself being treated like a cancer. You can reveal yourself to be not at all a cancer.

Many of us in the west are taking risks to prevent the further broadening of our battle with terrorists into a battle between cultures. You too must step up and take risks to outnumber and "outvoice" your radicals in order to help avoid a battle that could devastate civilization. We, moderates in the west **and** moderates within Islam, must work together to narrow the conflict. We are working on our side… you must work on your side. You can continue to monitor our words and our actions (including our votes). Show us with your words and actions that we can count on you too. At this point many of us are still convinced that you do <u>want</u> to avoid a disastrous conflict. Let's share that goal, and actively work towards it! If either of us fail, it will get very ugly and tragic for all of humanity.

It is worth remembering that our best chance at having some degree of logic prevail, at limiting the radical impulse for war, is when things are the least stressed. This puts urgency on our mission. **It is human nature that when things look scariest and most hopeless, more people resort to irrational beliefs, be they cultural or religious or both. If we keep creeping closer to all-out cultural war, it will get harder and harder to avoid.** <u>Now</u> it the time for clear thinkers to step up and help our respective cultures step back from the brink.

POST-SCRIPT TO MUSLIMS

If by any chance you have only read these few pages addressed to you, you will have the mistaken impression that I am promoting nothing but typical anti-Islamic propaganda. If you now go back and read the first two chapters of this book in their entirety you will discover quite the opposite. Please read the whole before you reach any conclusions.

CHAPTER 3.
REFLECTIONS ON LEADERSHIP

In looking at the world we find ourselves in with a focus on how we can affect the battle with terrorism, we would do well to think seriously about how cultural or national leaders affect the fights the people find themselves in. What characteristics or tendencies of leaders may help maximize chances of a stable and peaceful world, and what characteristics do the opposite? Do personal belief systems make leaders any more or less prone to put us all at risk of war? How would any particular leader identify the most important thing anyone needs to know about him, and what does that itself say about him? What are we willing to follow? Where and how far are we willing to go?

Of course we all have a tendency to follow leaders who articulate positions we personally subscribe to, but let's attempt to suspend personal attachment for a moment in objectively analyzing where those positions, applied to public and foreign policy, might take us.

Obviously people tend to vote for and follow leaders whom they think, at least for the moment, are correct in the positions they advocate. But a good question to ask ourselves might be "What if our leaders turn out to be wrong in some of their basic assumptions and positions? Are there intrinsic risks to certain positions?"

Let's apply this to some positions on a few of the sides surrounding our battle with terrorism. On one side we have fundamentalist Muslim leadership, represented by Osama bin Laden and perhaps some radical Mullahs. The most important thing they would want you to know about them is that they are true believers in Islam. They believe they are called to take over the world for Allah. If you were a regular Muslim citizen of some country evaluating whether or not these are leaders worth following, you would benefit from going through the following thought sequence: If he happens to be right, spreading Islam by the sword will work out ok in the end. Yes infidels will suffer, but that's ok you say because you think they should suffer. And if you and yours suffer and die in the cause of right, that will work out ok in the long run too.

The thought sequence continues. What if they are not right? Is death and destruction on all sides something that should at least trouble you? The world as a whole, and all of humanity including your own people will have suffered because you chose to follow leaders who didn't look at the big picture, who were so sure of their rightness that they went for destruction over the basic values of human rights.

Let's look for a moment now at some of our fundamentalist Christian leaders. They too are sure of what they believe, and many would say that the most important thing about them is their faith in God. They see Jesus Christ coming back to save true believers from an earthly mess. Some of them tend not to worry one iota about the environment because "We're only going to be here for a little while longer." Many of them believe in a world-ending Apocalypse. Again, the same thought sequence ought to be instructive. If they're right, everything will work out ok for us, Christian believers.

But what if they're wrong? All of humanity will inherit a worse environment, and if we willingly walk into an apocalyptic scenario, imagine how many will die needlessly because we, like our current enemies, let religious conviction enter into and direct how we conduct foreign policy.

Some might leap to the conclusion that I am advocating electing only atheist leaders. No way! I am simply advocating asking, "How high up the list of self-description does a leader's religious faith fit?" If it is at or very near the top, following that person means we are embracing risks that go along with seeing life through one unique tint of shaded glasses... ones that could turn out to be wrong.

We can indeed continue to elect people of faith. Many have a religiously based belief system, but a tempered one. A belief system that recognizes faith as faith, and that it includes a 'leap.' This type of person recognizes the equal validity of other faiths, and is careful to keep the perspective of their faith separate from judgements of best pragmatic and principled policy.

Let's apply the same test to the leader who's faith ranks much lower on the scale of self-description, who holds his faith with more humility and with less absolute certainty. If this type of leader applies his broad and relatively secular view, we and all of humanity stand our best chance for quality survival because unnecessary religiously driven wars are avoided. And what if they were wrong in making decisions based on their best assessment of the long-term good of our country and humanity as a whole without any particular religious perspective? Well, whichever "God" turns out to be right will still salvage and save what He wanted to anyway, so no unnecessary harm will have been done.

It may be worth noting that our historic tendency to trust politicians of faith is a bit of a funny thing. Have we learned anything from the Priest – pedophile tragedies? It should be obvious that the outward manifestations of religiosity, be they clothing or talk, are no guarantee of good character. Indeed, there are recent examples from within politics where avowed Christians were taking bribes, intimidating colleagues, and otherwise behaving in obviously un-Christ-like ways.

One hopes that in an educated and reflecting society we would begin to realize that:

 # 6. The faith of a politician should be a side issue… as long as it isn't among his top self-descriptors; at that point it becomes a risk.

The tendency to strongly and narrowly <u>believe</u> in one's faith has often been mistaken for personal confidence, a characteristic we like in leaders. Notice though that the confidence that makes one closed to new information and alternate points of view is actually much shallower than the personal confidence that makes one able to be open to new information and points of view. In truth:

 # 7. Real confidence is based in knowing <u>how</u> best to continue to figure things out and wisely adjust to realities in life, not simply in knowing <u>what</u> you believe now and forever.

I find myself hoping that one day soon we will elect presidents who will choose to include in their innermost circle of advisors a person with whom they very often disagree, but for whom they have deep respect.

A president with the confidence to expose his ideas to strong and informed criticism, and to listen carefully to and think deeply on other points of view would be much less prone to enormous errors that have lasting consequences and may take generations to reverse. It is up to us to reject leaders with shallow confidence and false bravado, and to elect leaders with sufficiently deep confidence to be able to remain open to perspectives they didn't happen to grow up with and may not initially like. We, voters, must begin to tell the difference between the two types of confidence.

CHAPTER 4.

THEATER OF THE ABSURD

In the chapter on the role of religion in our current conflict, when dealing with the simple truth that we are a secular nation we looked specifically at common arguments that have been used against the secular idea. Though I don't want to get sidetracked into an everyday blog of arguments about what our involvement in Iraq has done to our battle with terrorism, the fact that there are quite a few common arguments attempting to justify our being there which are so seriously flawed they approach the absurd motivates me to look specifically at them too.

Some have said that one of the reasons we haven't been able to secure a fairly quick win in Iraq is because we haven't been ruthless enough. They've said that nice guys finish last, and that pacifists die at the hands of the aggressive. You would think from this argument that we won WWII by being more ruthless than the Japanese or Germans. We can be proud of the fact that we weren't. Indeed, sometimes truth and right can prevail with the necessary toughness and perseverance, but without ruthlessness.

Some quickly argue that we were ruthless in bombing the heck out of the Germans and A-bombing the Japanese, civilians included. We did the necessary degree of ruthlessness, but our behavior on the whole was civilized. That I know of, we forced no death marches and had no extermination camps. More to the point though, the enemies we battled were whole, united populations… nations. We had to fight them all because they were all out to get us.

It is very different now. There are extremist segments who are out to get us, but they do not represent whole nations or cultures. We must fight those extremists, not only physically but mentally. We must be smart enough to not draw in the whole culture that surrounds the extremists. If you are one who accepts the idea that the whole Muslim culture must be fought, you are buying into an impossible fight. History demonstrates that you cannot eliminate a religion. A major factor in the growth of the early Christian church was persecution. The more you persecute any people of faith, the more their faith will grow… it's just that way. We don't have to be on the dumb end of that lesson again. With wisdom, toughness, selectivness, and perseverance we can fight terrorism without unnecessarily and mistakenly drawing in a whole culture.

An incredible irony of the argument in favor of

a more ruthless approach is that out of the self-same mouths have come comments like this being a battle of ideas, and this being a potential turning point in history. It **is** a battle of ideas. As often expressed, it is a battle for hearts and minds, and it has every possibility of being a turning point in history... that is the driving force for my writing. The question that I trust we recognize crying out for an answer is: Can we honestly hope to win a battle of ideas by being the most ruthless?!

The ruthless idea brings to mind the media battles over alleged and apparent war atrocities committed by a few of our forces. I trust we civilians keep in mind that most of us don't have a clue what it's like to be in a firefight where a moment's hesitation could cost you your life. I also trust that our forces keep foremost in their minds that we must maintain (or try to regain) the moral high ground. We can make lasting enemies in a moment's indiscretion; it can take generations to build trusting friendships. Unfortunately we have given our troops an almost impossibly tall order in trying to "maintain" the higher moral ground because we are where we shouldn't be to begin with.

Another convoluted argument begins with the idea that in the fight with terrorism we need a "front" that is somewhere specific, and we don't want it here. So far, so good. Some connect to this the idea that Saddam Hussein was a Hitler wanna-be, that our battle in Iraq is like WWII, and that if we didn't take him on he would have marched progressively outward. To this some add the notion that our being in Iraq is like us helping defend England against Hitler. Some push it still further in saying that we can use Iraq as a critical beachhead nation from which we can launch a counter-offensive in attempting to retake territory under the bad-guy's control.

We will have to come back to the above paragraph in several parts. First, yes, Saddam was a Hitler wanna-be, he was and is one bad dude. But his expansionist ideas were dealt an appropriate blow in the Gulf War of 1990, lead by the senior George Bush and a broad coalition. Oh Saddam still had bad wishful dreams, but under the watchful eye of the international community and effective no-fly zones, that's essentially all they were. Can we really run around imposing our will because we think (and have good reason to) that some leader is a bad guy? **Does force-feeding our version of democracy, whether the prerequisites to stable democracy are in place or not, make it an appealing and effective diet… or a despised foreign thing?**

Second, the battle in Iraq can't be remotely compared to WWII for numerous reasons. In WWII we had long-time allies begging and pleading for us to get out of our isolationist mode and get involved. Before Iraq we had allies initially urging caution and then flat out distancing themselves from us. Before WWII we had German u-boats sinking many of our merchant marine fleet and then Japan attacking Pearl Harbor; WWII was clearly *not* a war of choice, Iraq even more clearly *was*. Further, virtually everyone in England wanted us there helping them avoid being conquered by an aggressive foreign invader; the contrasts with Iraq shouldn't need more enumerating.

The most enormous error though is skirted around so often that many seem to forget it. Notice that the arguments three paragraphs back entangle the war on terror with the war in Iraq. We already had a specific front in the war on terror... Afghanistan. Sadaam was not in bed with al Qaeda; that didn't make him trustworthy, but it did and still does mean we didn't have the same universally accepted justification for invading Iraq as we did Afghanistan.

An irony of the WWII comparisons involves remembering how grateful England, ourselves, and all the allies can be that Hitler lost focus on the battle of Britain and opened up the front with Russia. That dilution and dispersal of German forces was incalculably costly to them. **No doubt al Qaeda is equally grateful for our opening up the front in Iraq.** The biggest reason for their gratitude though goes far beyond diluting our forces. **The difference it made and will make for some time to come in their recruiting ability is where the**

real pay-off for them lies. As pointed out in chapter one, many Muslims/Arabs who might have stayed as relative moderates, when faced with a bullying giant who was forcing his way where he now didn't have just cause, began to drift into the arms of extremists. We can only thank the lack of reasonable insight and foresight on the part of too many of our own ideologues.

So can Iraq, under our control or influence, serve as a launch point for our war on terror? In reality:

 # 8. If our presence is perceived as unjustified by the Muslim world, as is the case with Iraq but wasn't with Afghanistan, we are probably serving to recruit more future terrorists than we are killing today. Is that a winning formula?

We desperately need to achieve some reasonable level of stability in Iraq, and then get the heck out! An apology for mistaken judgement, even if it has to come from the next administration, might also do something toward reducing a major al Queda recruiting tool. Here's hoping.

A major part of the bottom line is simply that:

 # 9. We can't run around deposing dictators we don't like. In imposing our will around the world, what would that make us?

This doesn't mean we have to sit idly by while various forms of Kosovo, Rwanda, or Darfur are repeated in unnumbered places. For one, where there are clear, massive, humanitarian crises created by bad regimes, it will be broadly recognized by the clear majority of nations, and we could form a coalition of more than a handful. Most importantly, we wouldn't be viewed as bullying and serving our own interests, as long as we didn't stay and dictate nation-building our way for our gain. Secondly, **we can in fact be involved in spreading democracy, not by force, but by working with people to create the prerequisite conditions.** The difference this could make in mineral-rich but almost middle-classless countries where Jihadists recruit so effectively would be great. This would not mean eliminating existing governments, but rather working with them to develop their educational systems and broaden the economic base of activity.

I can't possibly address all the hawkish arguments in favor of our fight in Iraq. The fact is that ideologues will no-doubt keep coming up with new variations on the theme while trying to justify it. My hope is simply that more and more of us will begin to thoughtfully analyze the underpinnings of our recent foreign policy, and assert our voices, demanding decisions based on logic, evidence, and breadth of vision, not just beliefs.

Section II:

America's Durable Internal Stability

From this point on, the simple truths I present have nothing to do with the immediate urgency of dealing with a world affected by terrorism. Rather they have to do with attempting to look down the long road for our nation and culture, and for humanity as a whole. As mentioned in the preface, in twenty years we will hit the 250 year mark. These twenty years will bring plenty of challenges. Assuming we navigate those successfully, we need to begin thinking more and more of what will be good for our great grandchildren, and their great grandchildren. In fact, part of what may well help us get through the next twenty years intact could be that we begin now to think and act with the long run in mind. What we want <u>now</u>, politically and otherwise, can't continue to be the driving force behind our decisions. If we get better at thinking of what we want for our grandchildren we might realistically imagine that our descendents may one day be approaching the celebration of 500 years for our democracy.

Interestingly, while we view the world in a competitive way as we must, it is likely true that what is really good for America in the long run, will also be good for the rest of the world, and vice-versa. Thus we need to not only think of the best good of our children's children, but also of humanity as a whole. No, we don't want one world government, but we do want a stable world. If we think and act only for the immediate and only for ourselves, the world at large is likely to become a decidedly less stable place.

To bring us back home in our focus though, let's for the moment remember that part of winning against terrorism means we must avoid a power vacuum in the world at large, which means that America's strength (and wisdom in using it) is needed. Further, broad economic and social stability at home is part of what is needed in order to maintain America's strength.

Economic and social stability involve many things. I suggest that our educational system is fairly obviously a key component. Further, science education in particular is important both because of its role in maintaining our technological capabilities and because it so happens that science education is where part of the battle over religion's place in our nation is being waged. The difference between objectively analyzing evidence and reasserting cherished beliefs is critical, and has an affect not only directly in scientific endeavors but also in applied social and political policy.

A third very important area in maintaining economic and social stability at home involves fiscal policy, and taxes/spending. A balanced budget, based on a thorough review of realistic expectations and with a view to the good of our whole society, is desperately needed.

I cannot possibly deal with every significant issue which influences our economic and social stability at home, but in the chapter titled "Potpourri" I have chosen to deal with a few in addition to the three mentioned above. These include: Immigration, how Soft and Spoiled we are getting, Energy, and Affirmative Action and Race Relations.

Again, join the discussion.

CHAPTER 5.

EDUCATION

Working for nearly a decade in a private Christian educational system and now for a decade in public education has given me more than my share of exposure to discussions of what's wrong and what's right in American education. Some of the most interesting observations and comments have come though, from outside the system. One remark I've heard more than once goes something like "We'll fund education to a better degree when they improve performance and put out a better product."

When I've asked whether they expect to get improved performance by shifting class sizes from 25 to 35, particularly at the elementary level, they've looked a little surprised and uncomfortable. The topic then inevitably shifts to administrative waste etc. I, like any sane person, readily acknowledge the need for greater efficiency and the cutting of duplicated administrative (federal, state, local) costs. This particular discussion serves to bring into focus two particularly important aspects of education: student performance and funding.

The ability to compare, based on first-hand experience, private and public education has been informative to me. My students in parochial schools were no smarter on average, but I do have a much higher rate of sustained failure in public schools. Why? When I sent home an "F" to parents who were paying hard cash for their child's education, something happened. Failure didn't continue. In public schools I have sent home "F"s for six consecutive grading periods, and sadly in most cases nothing ever changed. The difference had to do with what parents would put up with, what standard of expectation they set, and how they supported and reinforced their child's efforts.

This perfectly matches what I concluded at the end of my first year in public education, a year in which I was a substitute teacher. Having been reared in parochial schools, my extended family had many long-held reservations about public schools. When, at the end of that year of subbing, one family member asked me about the evils we had all feared in public schools I was able to reply, "There are lost kids going nowhere, dropping out. There are also kids who have their act completely together. Some going on scholarships to top-flight universities, some are doing great things in their home communities. And you know what? They've all gone through the same classrooms and schools. They've all had the same teachers. So what has made the difference? The home; what was expected, and what was supported."

This brings me to my first simple truth in education.

#10. It not only takes effort on the part of teachers and schools, it takes effort and support beyond the school to ensure that kids get good educations and that their performances improve.

Yes, the leverage I have as a teacher on a low performing student is limited. I can be thorough, I can set a high standard, I can be creative. Shoot, I can stand on my head and do the hoola. But I can't match the leverage that somebody at home setting some basic expectations can exert.

The irony here is that public schools have been made the whipping boys for poor performance, and most of this has come from the end of the political spectrum that often preaches personal accountability. This is a broader societal issue. What can we do to hold children and parents accountable for their efforts and performance?

We don't need and don't want more big government, but we might benefit from broadening the discussion. Should various social benefits continue to go to the homes of under-performing students? Could after-school programs be required in some circumstances? Where would the funding for supplemental programs come from?

#11. Like life in general, in education you tend to get what you pay for.

The far right has got some competing and contradictory agendas going in education. The emphasis on cutting taxes without regard to consequences has led to nearly a decade of declining funding in education. One of the immediate consequences has been progressively larger class sizes. There is research that shows the importance of lower class size to student performance, but who really needs it? Surely it meets the common sense test to recognize that more can be accomplished with each individual student in a room full of 22 third graders than can be accomplished in a room full of 32 third graders.

It really lacks common sense and is unrealistic to force larger class sizes while demanding improved performance. Hello!

One of the longer-term consequences of under-funding education may not come home to roost for a little while yet, but I deem it worth mentioning now. While the echo of the echo of the baby boom begins coming through our schools, the number of teachers seems on the decline. What about recruiting more? Well, from time to time teachers have students ask them, "What do you feel about a career in education? Are you glad you became a teacher?" And most of us (I trust) can honestly answer, "Yes." But when the questions go on and get more detailed, we have to concede things like, "Yes, you can make more in almost any field with equivalent years of training and preparation." The trouble is that the sharp students, who are aware of the world, and perhaps a touch more materially minded than before, know that it is "substantially" more in a wide array of fields.

Does the future of education bode well if we become progressively less able to attract at least some of the best and the brightest? Raising the overall quality of teachers means having standards of acceptance in college education programs that go well beyond warm bodies. We also need to limit the number of times a candidate can try to pass the various tests of basic knowledge/skills to become a teacher. Yet either of those steps would further limit the number of teachers coming out. A major part of the solution to that, to making becoming a teacher a more competitive process while still turning out more teachers, is to make the profession more attractive to more talented young people. Are we doing that with perpetual under-funding?

#12. Various aspects of "No Child Left Behind" and other federal mandates, including some involving "Highly Qualified" teachers, are unattainable or impractical goals.

Schools take in kids with the **full** range of abilities and backgrounds. To say that 100% of those kids, special ed., brand new English-language-learners, etc. are going to pass various standardized tests is simply setting frustratingly unachievable goals for the students, parents, and teachers. If that 100% success mark was reached by even the slowest learners and the least prepared, wouldn't it simply be an indication that the bar was set so low that it would be a meaningless measure of "success" for the bulk of students? It's rather like wishing that everybody in the country was in sufficient cardiovascular health to be able to cover a mile in under eight minutes, but since they aren't and can't, let's lower the standard to fifteen minutes.

Further, smaller rural schools will be able to offer fewer and fewer electives when teachers cannot teach a subject or two beyond their official endorsement areas. Who is being served when, for political reasons, laws are made that limit what electives are available to students in small-school rural America?

13. **The huge emphasis on pulling up the performance of our low and marginal students is taking time and effort away from talented and or motivated students.**

If the parents of talented or motivated students, or for that matter average students, could sit in class and see the level of effort and time spent on clarification, re-explanation, re-illustration, etc. that goes on in the name of pulling up the lowest students in an effort to help them meet the minimum standards, they would be appalled. I used to feel confident that we were able to prepare the talented or motivated kids to compete in university programs with privileged kids from elite private schools. Now our talented or motivated are to an even greater degree "on their own" when it comes to getting the most out of their high school education. If this trend continues, the gap between their prep experience and that of the privileged elite could become so large that I don't know if any but the extreme exception will be able to compete.

This is perhaps the **most important point** to be made on the current trend in education and our ability to stay strong and stable as a culture and nation. **We can't let a superficially commendable focus on the lowest groups keep public education from doing a thorough and quality job on the talented and motivated.** The end result of the current emphasis will be an almost permanent elite who, generation after generation, get their university preparation in private schools. Not everything or every group can be <u>the</u> top priority. Balanced emphasis would accept the reality that some may choose failure, and let us return some resources and effort where it may make the biggest difference.

#14. Anybody and everybody, however poorly educated their home background, can see the simple reality that putting effort into doing well in school opens up doors of opportunity in their future, and conversely, that dinging around and failing in school is going to result in unskilled and low-paying jobs.

The point here is not the fact that doors of opportunity are opened or shut based on one's level of achievement in school, rather, it is that **everybody does know this fact.** There is choice involved. Remember the good old expression "You can lead a horse to water, but you can't make it drink!" Again, it is ironic that the group that generally puts the most vocal emphasis on personal accountability has led the charge in blaming "failing" schools.

Teachers can be expected to be well prepared, to be thorough, to be creative, to be fair, to work at motivating, to never give up on anyone or any group, to be professional, to set high standards, and to lead by example, but they can't be expected to **make** anyone learn. People can and unfortunately do choose to remain undereducated and ignorant. Interestingly, one can even argue that there is a place in the economy for unskilled labor, and that it really doesn't have to be all illegally imported, but that is its own topic for another chapter.

I'm not arguing that everyone has the maturity to make wise choices when they are 16, let alone 10. I'm simply pointing out that no matter how lamentable their choice, and no matter how hard teachers work to help students eventually make different choices, in the end teachers and schools can't actually force wise choices on their students.

The bottom line is that we need an educational philosophy and governmental expectations which acknowledge the role of personal choice, and a system which doesn't insist that all students follow the university prep track. No matter how enormous a role information and technology eventually play in our economy, we will still have a diverse job base and the need for differing levels of skill.

CHAPTER 6.

SCIENCE EDUCATION

Continuing in education, but shifting gears...

The public debate over how best to teach science, specifically how to deal with evolution and whether intelligent design should be part of science or not, is obviously a very hot button. Again, I cover this topic with a good degree of reluctance because some feel so intensely about it, but I discuss this issue anyway in the hope of helping us think and act based on clear thinking and not on hot emotion.

My career in education, both in private and in public schools, has been spent almost entirely in the field of science. I taught biology in Christian schools, and I teach it now in public school. I could deal with this in a dry way, but that only glosses over the depth of feelings involved; so, I am choosing to deal with it by sharing some of what I've experienced and learned along the way.

Before I became a teacher I obviously was a student, and I came up through Christian schools. What I learned about evolution and the fossil record was basically that any "pattern" or "sequence" was the result of selective perception or outright invention on the part of dishonest or deceptive atheist scientists. Among the criticisms directed at these evolutionists was that they formed their conclusions ahead of time and simply went about selecting evidence and creating theoretical explanations to support their prior conclusions. Once out of high school and into a Christian college in the mid 1970s, I learned that over the previous several decades conservative Christian scientists had moved away from denying the pattern and sequence in the fossil record. Rather, they had begun attempting to explain the sequence that was increasingly clear and undeniable.

I began to be exposed to literature put out by the Geoscience Research Institute (GRI), a conservative Christian organization founded in 1958 to find scientific support for traditional Biblical views of earth's history. I continued to read publications from this and other conservative sources, and while working as a biology teacher at a Christian high school in the mid 1980s had the privilege of being part of a weekend seminar lead by Dr. Robert Brown, then chairman of GRI. One question that was put to him sticks out clearly in my memory. A science professor at a Christian college asked, "Is there any type of evidence, in any amount, which would convince you that evolution has actually happened?"

His answer is equally clear in my memory. After a moment's pause he said, "No. My faith in what I believe is too strong." There were amens and heads that nodded in agreement, but a few of us shared puzzled expressions. While continuing to read conservative literature, I had allowed myself to read more broadly and by then was quite acquainted with a wide array of raw scientific evidence that bore on the topic. Even an occasional student in my high school classes had pointed to weaknesses in conservative explanations of the fossil record.

Among explanations of the sequence of increasing complexity found in the fossil record was something called the "Ecological Zonation Theory." Basically it proposed that the sequence in the fossil record was the result of the Biblical flood which buried things in sequence according to where they lived, how mobile they were, and how intelligent they were in figuring out how best to escape rising flood-waters. This was all intended to explain in general why mammal and bird fossils are found above (after) reptiles, which are above amphibian, which are above fish. Of course it was noted that apes and humans are both smart and their fossilized remains aren't found until the very upper layers.

I remember a tall, thin student who had more interest in music than science, but who had clear insight. I had to concede to him, "You're right. Various mammals or birds which died in the decades and centuries before the

Biblical flood story could easily have been buried, and the occasional one fossilized in lower layers… yes even down there with the invertebrates." The fact that we don't find scattered glaring exceptions to the obvious sequence spelled trouble to that attempt to explain the fossil record.

Others' attempts to explain things have picked on terminology and tried to avoid the evidence for evolution by saying that species can adapt (micro-evolution) but that major change (macro-evolution) hasn't happened. A thorough look at the fossil record of whale evolution from land dwelling mammals provides convincing evidence (follow their limbs, hips, and skulls) that macro-evolution does happen. Some would argue that this is still within mammals, and so it is; but one can also check the evidence for amphibian's ancestors being fish, and the bird-reptile connection.

Other ingenious and sometimes desperate attempts to explain the evidence have been made. One of the most creative I've heard proposes that the flood did indeed create a relatively chaotic fossil record like one would expect. But then the devil and his angels saw an opportunity to deceive future generations of man into thinking that there was a pattern which showed a sequence of evolutionary change, so they got right into the messy mud of the flood aftermath and arranged the fossils. My students have always recognized that we can't prove or disprove that explanation; with a smile we can simply acknowledge that it is "possible."

The difference though between possible and probable/logical becomes important. It is possible that I'm nothing more than a worm off in space with a vivid imagination; I imagine my family, my work, even my writing this. It's also possible that you, the reader, are the worm off in space with the vivid imagination; you imagine your family, your work, and reading this. So let's get over what's possible, and begin to really look at what's probable and logical.

I found it troubling that the very accusation leveled at evolutionists, that they form their conclusions ahead of time and selectively look for or create data which supports their theories, turned out to be so overwhelmingly true of my then-fellow conservatives. When I finally admitted that I had been part of the reaching and stretching to either ignore or distort the real data, I knew I had to quit teaching science within a conservative Christian school context. I have since simply tried to follow the philosophy of letting the data almost speak for itself; interpret it in the simplest and most direct way possible. This isn't easy; we all have a natural tendency to see and believe what we happen to want to. To fight this tendency I have come to a mantra that I think is actually broadly applicable: **Evidence Matters.** And yes, it matters more than what may have been my previously held most cherished beliefs.

This brings me to the first simple truth in this controversial field.

#15. The simplest and most direct explanation of the evidence of the fossil record, of comparative molecular biology (both DNA and amino acid sequences), of comparative anatomy, of geographic distribution, and of comparative embryology is evolution by natural selection.

When introducing evolution to my current classrooms full of public school students who are predominantly from conservative homes, I am careful to help them note exactly what evolution means. It means change over time. I am also careful to note what it does not mean. It does not mean, despite what some insist, anything one way or the other about God. I try to set them at ease by assuring them that if they don't believe in God, fine, they won't get an argument from me; if they do believe in God, fine, they won't get an argument from me. What they believe about God is none of my business, and religion isn't part of what we do in science class. We do science, we do actual evidence.

After going through the various types of evidence showing that indeed things have changed over time (including the mass extinctions and subsequent explosions of diversity) and seeing that things evidently do have ancestral histories, we come to the point of ultimate origins of the first cells. Some of my science colleagues would condemn me for wimping out, but at this point I try to leave my individual students with the freedom to think what they happen to want to about a leap that we can't demonstrate either way (either cells did arise from progressively more complex molecules or they were created). We don't discuss it; I simply acknowledge that we can't do real science with "ultimate origins" and so we skip it. Personally, I'd rather we were helping create a generation which had developed the skill of reasonably interpreting real hard evidence, and that we not force young people into buying into the idea that the first cell just happened (abiogenesis and atheism). When forced to that point I think many students just emotionally rebel at the thought and throw the baby (evolution by natural selection) out with the bath water (possibly the case for atheism).

I try to reassure my students that if they absolutely want and need to have a god, that there is no proof there isn't one. I further inform them that some people, even some with Ph.D.s in science, find personally satisfying and widely creative ways of accepting the evidence for evolution while still believing in a god of some type.

With what I've described in the last few paragraphs some may conclude that I am an advocate of teaching intelligent design. I am not. While I don't see a problem in acknowledging that we can't demonstrate hard evidence on how the first cells came about, I see significant short-comings in our level of understanding of natural selection when we resort to saying that all manner of complex organs must have been created from scratch. It may require some major revamping of our preconceptions, but natural selection is an amazing process in itself and there is little serious question, and no real lack of evidence, that it can progressively modify and continue to improve on previous "models." Why not try to understand the mechanism behind a complex process? After all, that is a major part of what science is about.

Our long-ago ancestors accepted many things as magic or divine. If humanity had just always continued to accept simple or amazing processes as magic we would not only be doing without computers, cars, and refrigerators, but we'd also be surviving in crude shelters with no indoor hot running water. Remember that while enjoying a refreshing, warm, and cleansing shower and it adds a little appreciation for the process of scientific inquiry, and for early scientists.

But it does take time to get over certain key preconceptions. Before Nicholas Copernicus worked through the evidence carefully enough to come up with a model that put the sun at the center and explained the motion of the then-known planets, everyone accepted what appeared to be obvious. The church, conservative Christianity of its day, wasn't alone in stating that the earth is at the center, that the sun is what moves as it "rises and sets," and that the earth is flat. Shoot, just look around; doesn't that fit the apparent evidence, agree with scripture, and wasn't it intuitively appealing (just like intelligent design) to regular folk and church-goers alike? It took a couple of centuries for this new heliocentric idea to finally gain broad acceptance and for churches and individuals to get over the feeling that their faiths were being swept away.

Although Darwin proposed his idea of evolution by natural selection a century and a half ago now, the public at large has only been really dealing with the idea for not quite a century yet. No, the case for evolution is not a complete slam dunk; there probably never will be irrefutable proof. But yes, the evidence continues to mount. Scientists well this side of Darwin had no idea how well DNA and amino acid sequences would reveal degrees of relatedness. And the "problem" with absent transitional forms (missing links) is turning out to be a strength as every decade reveals more and more previously absent but newly discovered forms that fit in where predicted. Still, that doesn't change the fact that it is going to take some time to accept it like we eventually accepted the earth not being at the center, and to get over being threatened by it.

(If you find yourself resistant to but curious about the notion of evolution, I would suggest you read the cover article in the November 2004 National Geographic. It is not anti-God, and it does a fairly good job of giving the reader an overview of the evidence.)

During the time it takes for our culture to work this through, we might do well to be a little bit patient with each other. While we're patient, we still need to be careful though. Blurring religious beliefs into science class is a mistake at least in part because it arrests a fundamental part of what science is about... the search to understand natural mechanisms. Keeping religion-based assertions out of the science classroom not only should place some constraints on the science teacher who happens to be an evangelical Christian (he shouldn't push his belief in God), it also places some constraints on the science teacher who happens to be a convinced atheist (he shouldn't push his belief that there is no god).

In summary, my last simple truth related to science education.

#16. Intelligent Design might be taught in a philosophy class, but it should not be taught in science because it short-cuts the key scientific process of seeking to understand natural mechanisms and it introduces articles of "faith" where "questioning" should be standard procedure.

It is too bad that issues like this have to end up in court, but a couple of centuries from now I think people will look back on the uproar rather like we look back on the fight over whether the sun or the earth is at the center. I've been reassured to see the collective wisdom of the voters in Dover, PA, who, despite many of them holding religious beliefs, spoke clearly at the ballot box in saying that they can take care of religious beliefs outside of the science classroom. Yes, let science be science.

Most importantly in the big picture, whatever we each take as articles of faith, let's not mistake them for science, and let's take them with sufficient humility so as to not drag ourselves or our nation into wasting resources or engaging in cultural conflict or war to prop up our particular faiths. I like to think that good science education can help us avoid this type of waste and conflict. If we apply the mantra that **Evidence Matters,** even more than our cherished preconceptions, to any potential war situation, it may well make a difference in our decisions on that conflict.

CHAPTER 7.

POTPOURRI
(Immigration Policy, Soft and Spoiled, Energy, and Affirmative Action)

If I have upset members of the "right" in my previous chapters, by the end of this chapter I'll be taking arrows from two directions because I know that a lot of what I say in this section will upset those on the "left." So be it. Again, the hope is that we in the middle will increasingly speak up and limit the influence of the squeaky extremes.

In areas like these I don't bring any particular professional or experiential expertise; rather, I will take what I consider to be a common sense approach. Obviously there is room for debate. I speak up, despite knowing I will take some fire, simply because these are important areas that I believe will affect the long-term stability and strength of our nation.

IMMIGRATION

The current situation of lax border enforcement and lax "legal laborer/ legal employer" enforcement is a long-term recipe for disaster. I don't know the details in this field, so I'll be brief. Business seems addicted to access to cheap labor, but illegal cheap labor is a problem, and it's a problem largely of our own making. We Americans, from home-owners with yard work to business owners large and small, who have wanted to do things on the cheap without regard to broad consequences or basic legality have had the largest part in making the bed we are now complaining about lying in. Business throws around the excuse that if they couldn't hire such cheap labor, the price of all kinds of products and services would have to passed on to consumers. Hello. What's wrong with that? I tend to believe that our economy can absorb reality.

The spin-off costs of illegal immigration are wide-ranging and enormous. Why should tax paying American citizens support the health care, welfare, and education of people who have no right to **be** here, let alone a right to those services? We should note here though that if we continue to turn a blind eye to their coming and working here because we like being able to hire cheap labor, then we are users if we don't let them benefit from the economy they help support.

It's also worth noting that we probably do have the necessary laborers-in-the-making right here at home. If not every one of our American students choose to succeed on the university prep track, shouldn't there be a demand in the economy for homegrown laborers, and shouldn't we be able and willing to pay the lowest end of our labor force a wage sufficient to support a decent, if decidedly non-luxurious, living?

Will it be easy to wake up, smell the coffee, and start enforcing all relevant aspects of legal immigration? This obviously must include not only strong border enforcement but also strong penalties for Americans trying to hire on the cheap. No it won't be easy, but I believe that in the long run it will turn out to be worth it.

Interestingly, while there may be some in the Hispanic community who feel that there is racism behind any move to tighten illegal immigration, it is members of the legal Hispanic community (who have as much right to be here as any of us; many of whom **are** American citizens) who have the most to gain by enforcing the legality of being here. For starters, wages for the less skilled would no longer be depressed by the ready availability of workers who have no legal recourse against unfair employers. This benefit to the legal Hispanic community is broadly true under normal circumstances, but other benefits most would be unaware of could become significant should we come under extreme circumstances.

Let me illustrate extreme circumstances. I have lived where resource competition and economic survival stress merged with previously low-level ethnic tension and reached a breaking point, and it was horrific. I refer to Rwanda and what happened in 1994. Before making the point I want to, let me assure you that I am well aware that the chaos that exploded around us there was multi-factorial, and that because our whole country is much more educated, we are at substantially less risk of degenerating into that degree of madness.

Here is a significant part of what happened there. We had a country of 8 million people, with not even a half million of those people living in significant villages, the eight major towns, and the capital city <u>combined</u>! It was the most evenly spread rural population-base I have even seen. It was as if a giant hand holding a salt shaker of huts had shaken them across the countryside; you could have literally hit a golf ball from any hut to some other huts. While there was not the abject poverty found in huge cities in developing countries, few had any luxuries. Nearly everyone lived hand-to-mouth off the little land they cultivated. And, as of 1994, the average woman was still having over 7 children in her lifetime. As the population had boomed since the 1950s, families had simply progressively carved up the land they owned among their many children. A basic economic survival resource, land, was reaching a critical stress point.

Add to that basic scenario the following: a severely undereducated population (more subject to manipulation), a level of political stress from attempts to move toward multiparty democracy, and politicians more than willing to exploit an existing low level of ethnic suspicion and mistrust. Suddenly whole communities were whipped up to the point where mistrust had morphed into animalistic hatred. Oh, there were noteworthy islands of sanity, heroism, and even self-sacrifice. But basically, other societal dividing lines from church membership, to neighborhood, to marriage, to work association dissolved amidst ethnic tensions gone wild.

In America it is jobs, not land, which could most likely become the basic economic survival resource. Are there various ethnic stresses? Certainly. If uncontrolled demand for, acceptance of, and movement of illegal immigration continues, and then the economy takes a serious dive, we could be in for some rough and shameful times. Again, I firmly believe that our overall level of education would make us much less susceptible to manipulation by any crazy politician or radical member of the media, but I have seen enough violence in my time to have a healthy fear of what humans can devolve into when pushed to what is for them a breaking point. I am sure that there are unnumbered millions of Americans who made sure to have friendly casual conversations with fellow-Americans of middle-eastern descent following 9-11; we wanted them to know that we viewed them like any other American. Unfortunately there were also scattered cases where some fearful, reactionary, and bigoted citizen used the justified anti-terrorist environment as an excuse to lash out at some who just "looked" like the wrong ethnic group.

I trust that the overwhelming majority of any side of ethnic stress in America would take the side of right, and not participate in any hate-based intimidation or killing. But should we let uncontrolled immigration add to the various stresses that will be part of life when we do have economic tough times? And might I add to my fellow-Americans who happen to be of Hispanic origin, if you take the lead in calling for realistic, modernized, and <u>enforced</u> immigration policies, besides benefiting the most, won't you also have the most effective voice?

It may well be worth noting that the most effective aspect of enforcement probably isn't simply border security. If we really step up in our expectations of each other to always and only hire laborers who are legally here, and we back that up with <u>serious</u> penalties for doing otherwise, we would find millions of illegals actually heading back home voluntarily because they are out of work and can't find a job. Then, we would find the tide of new illegals drying up in a hurry... the lack of demand on this side would do more to stop the flow than anything else.

At the bottom line,

#17. The long-term economic and social health of our nation will be better off if we work to strictly limit immigration to legal immigration.

In the big picture, part of both the illegal immigration problem here and the atrocities committed in Rwanda have to do with uncontrolled population growth. Not only is our lack of "legal laborer" enforcement creating a magnet on our side of the border, but the continued steep population growth rate in Mexico creates emigration pressure there. I'm not saying it is our business to do something about on-the-ground family planning policy 'enforcement' in Mexico or any other developing nation, but I do believe that we need to be conscious of the problem, and begin to affect attitudes.

Looked at globally, addressing the population growth problem may well be one of the keys to humanity itself seeing all of us mark the passing of the next 250 years. If we make it that far without degenerating into chaos, we can make it much much deeper in time. One could easily connect a broad range of problems, from war to water pollution, from disease epidemic risk to global warming, all to the population situation, but that would be a needless side-track from the point at hand. We must also keep in mind that it is too easy for us in America to see the population challenge as something we have already controlled at home, and have no affect on in the world abroad.

Though we can't and shouldn't get involved in enforcement of family planning, we can be constructively engaged in encouraging the circumstances in which population stability tends to happen. Rather than expressing our incredulity at impoverished people having large families only to watch many of their children suffer and die, it is worth noting that we in the west benefited from reduced death rates (especially among the very young) <u>before</u> we brought birth rates down. That bears repeating: death rates come down first, then birth rates come down (as people develop confidence that their few children have every likely-hood of surviving, not only childhood, but into their old age).

What leads to low death rates? Some might think of modern health care systems, but a much more fundamental prerequisite could be termed basic quality of life. If you reflect on that for a moment you realize it encompasses employment, education, and the whole economic infrastructure.

As I mentioned in the introduction to Part II of this book, although we must accept the competitive nature of economic survival in the world, it is never-the-less true that **what is good for us in the long run necessarily takes into consideration what is good for humanity in a global sense.** They go together. It takes thinking beyond competitively.

Before commenting further on what we can do to help create population stabilizing circumstances, I am going to point out one thing that has had an adverse affect on bringing population growth into check. As a public health worker in Rwanda I made family planning a priority. I very quickly found out that 'access' wasn't as big a problem as 'attitudes'. There were local 'traditional' reasons for resistance to family planning, but in the middle of Africa the most frequently voiced objection was the Catholic church's official position against it.

I'm not Catholic bashing; I'm simply pointing out that a western based influence is making the global population situation, especially in developing nations, a bigger and longer-lasting problem. The same influence is significant in Mexico. What can we do about it? Regular citizens might feel like answering "nothing." I hope though, that we never underestimate the power of persistent people. Yes, the Vatican is ever so slow to change, but look at what average American Catholics have long-since put into practice in their own lives. They have seen for several generations that "Be fruitful and multiply" has been more than followed, and that other Biblical guidance also calls us to take good care of children and avoid needless suffering. Imagine millions of regular Catholics taking the lead in putting grass-roots pressure on the Vatican from within the church. Personally, I have to be hopeful.

Other aspects of creating the right circumstances for population stability most obviously include raising the quality of life and thereby lowering death rates (the first step). How do we most effectively engage ourselves in raising the quality of life in developing nations? It might be surprising to some, but hand-out aid is not the best way. One of the hardest lessons I had to learn in Rwanda (and have seen elsewhere) is that aid has to be channeled carefully and wisely or it will create dependence, not initiative and independence. We need to ensure open and fair trade. We need to invest where free and open markets make it possible. And we need to act with the knowledge that **the long-term good of the poor in developing countries is tied to our long-term good.**

SOFT AND SPOILED

A recurring theme in this book is the need for the here-to-fore too silent middle to become more active in setting public policy. In this section I'm not sure the public policy aspect applies to curing or reversing the imbalance of the sense of entitlement vs. practical reality, but the attitudes and actions of thinking mid-Americans certainly do apply. Though my concerns about us being so spoiled that we will fall apart from within focus somewhat on today's youth, this problem definitely crosses generations.

Unfortunately, too many young people today have a sense that life "should" continue to get easier, no matter that they don't want to work hard to make it happen. Too many don't want to put serious effort into school, but they still want to find a high paying job. Too many have no idea of how hard life was for those who endured the depression and World War II.

If circumstances drastically changed, I believe a new generation of tough survivors would emerge. But what if life doesn't suddenly change? What if we just gradually drift into ever greater personal and national debt and into deeper trade deficits? The possibilities for our economy and culture can be scary.

Even among an older generation of baby boomers who should have some closer connection to the real meaning of sacrifice and hardship, unrealistic expectations of entitlement can have broad and damaging affects on our sustainability. People bemoan the supposed shame of some having to choose between paying the heating bill and affording the multiple prescription drugs that keep them ticking. What sacred law or reasonable principle says that we as individuals or as a whole society can or should afford the potentially unlimited costs of keeping us alive? Is this question even more applicable when many of the chronic diseases that so burden us economically are often self-inflicted by poorly chosen and soft life-styles?

As I suggested at the beginning of this section, I'm

not sure there are policy solutions to these problems. There are though attitudinal and action solutions. Take for example the problem of agricultural harvest being so dependent on illegal labor. I have heard it asserted for decades now that if not for illegal migrant laborers, many fruit crops would just fall off the trees and rot. This is likely at least partially if not wholly true. The irony is that this is true while there are not-too-distant cities with numerous people on various welfare or unemployment programs.

Before we urban mid-Americans get too comfortable pointing fingers, perhaps we ought to ask ourselves if we have able-bodied pre-teens and teens who don't have full-time summer jobs. Imagine that orchardists had web-sites where I could sign up myself and two of my kids for a week or two "working vacation." For urban kids everywhere, a week or two of physical labor in harvesting a valuable crop would probably be a positive, profitable, and character-building experience. I suspect that we have the necessary labor force sitting around thinking or learning that life just happens for them. Is this one simple partial-solution meant to imply that the whole problem of agricultural harvest and our softness and dependence on illegal labor could be easily solved? Not at all. It is meant as an example of actually recognizing a problem, and then taking steps to address it. Often large solutions can be composed of many different partial-solutions. Where there's a will, there's a way.

Simply put,

#18. The combination of exporting our jobs and importing our laborers while expecting to maintain our lifestyle is non-sustainable pie-in-the-sky. We must re-value hard work and re-evaluate our expectations.

ENERGY

Some things are so obvious they don't even merit bold print. There is not an infinite supply of fossil fuels. With continued economic growth in much of the developing world the demand for petroleum is increasing, and is going to continue to. Limited supply plus increasing demand means ever-increasing prices. What's the solution? Increasing efficiency and increased utilization of an array of energy forms like solar, wind, and hydrogen fuel cells will help. Much more space could be dedicated to emphasizing the importance of developing these alternative energy sources, but I'm not going to spend time discussing things which I think most of us already agree on. I must point out though the one potentially large-scale energy source which we have been neglecting most: nuclear energy has been put on hold for longer than we can realistically afford.

Fear from experiences like Three Mile Island and Chernobyl has kept us with the brakes on, but we simply can't stay that way. This is one area where I think most of us can justifiably give President Bush some credit for being far-sighted.

Modern nuclear technology has been engineered to be very reliable and virtually fail-safe. I know, never say never, but it really can be incredibly safe. Add to that safety the basic pragmatic considerations of demand, low environmental impact, and long-term low cost and we might as well get back to developing these generating facilities <u>now</u> rather than waiting until we are truly desperate.

#19. Nuclear generated power is an essential part of our long-term energy viability, and the sooner, the more of it, the better.

As to drilling in Anwar, Alaska, the real issue should be that of timing. Some day we will absolutely need to drill because oil prices and our level of dependence on foreign oil will demand it. To some degree though, the further we can put it off, the better. I don't know how long it takes to get from agreeing, "Ok, we need to do this" to getting oil on line, but I imagine a few years would do it. Anwar then can act like a long-term strategic reserve. Exploit it too soon and we just continue our "live for today; tomorrow whatever" mentality. And then in some real tomorrow we have less of an economic buffer from what eventually could become the last major reserve on earth.

AFFIRMATIVE ACTION

To a great degree this is none of my business, and some might ask what this has to do with anything. I bring it up because, though minor, it is almost a reflection of some small issues that can be destabilizing to our broader society over the long haul.

Was affirmative action a necessary and good thing? Absolutely yes. Is it still? Possibly. Will it be indefinitely? Certainly not. The shameful blot that slavery and racism, both individual and institutional, cast on our national heritage is regrettable and undeniable. Affirmative action was an essential part of attempting to level the playing field of opportunity for which America stands. But I can easily imagine a day when talented and motivated black Americans would want to be recognized for their drive and achievement without any possibility of a perceived asterisk by it.

#20. Affirmative action has been a good thing, but its end should be in sight.

The question then is one of timing. Have we reached that day? I don't think quite. But should we within the next half century? One would think surely. This is really a debate that can most effectively be led by black Americans themselves, and many of them would stand to loose a stigma and gain one of the final steps to real equality. True equality of opportunity is one of the foundations on which the long-term stability of our nation and culture rests.

POST-SCRIPT ON RACE RELATIONS

Having dealt with illegal immigration and affirmative action, in which Hispanics and African Americans are naturally interested racial subgroups, I feel compelled to add a few clarifying remarks. The remarks I add though, are very definitely directed to each and every ethnic subgroup, whether they be Korean, Indian, or white.

An important question to ask ourselves is: Am I most interested in protecting and promoting people of my own ethnic group, or am I most interested in protecting and promoting American values? I will add some more pointed questions to this in a moment, but for now let's start by reminding ourselves of what core American values are.

Two simple words sum it up: freedom and equality. We have many freedoms, and among the most important of these is speech. Whatever our other differences on various values, we are free to discuss and debate them without fear because of freedom of speech. When we refer to equality, we all know we are not referring to the enforced "equality" of socialism, but to equality of opportunity.

As complimentary as freedom and equality are to each other, they still impose logical limits on each other. In order to avoid keeping a permanent underclass, or creating new ones, or defacto keeping a permanent ruling class, the freedom to pursue and keep wealth must be tempered by the American value of equality of opportunity. Notice that implied in equality of opportunity is the very basic idea of fairness. The unfortunate history of racism, whose aftermath we are still overcoming, illustrated the need to limit certain aspects of freedom in education, business contracts, etc. in order to advance the value of equality of opportunity, the idea of fairness. Yes, affirmative action was absolutely necessary.

What about today? I will first ask a pointed question to American Hispanics. On the question of legal vs. illegal immigration, do you favor ideas like blanket amnesty for illegals? Do you hope for continued weak borders? If so, why? If you find in your heart an inclination to favor policies (or the lack of policy) which favor your ethnic group over the basic American value of fairness, are you being an American or, in a way, racist? If you find yourself uncomfortable with the question and with your initial response, it is not hopeless. With rational analysis we all can work through beliefs which we may not even have realized we held. Progress is possible.

My second pointed question goes to whites. Can we recognize that the value of equality of opportunity made affirmative action a necessary positive action, and that we alone shouldn't be the only group to decide when it becomes unnecessary? Whether or not we harbor some degree of racism in our individual hearts may be best answered by asking ourselves if we would be completely comfortable, or not, with a child of ours marrying a person from another ethnic group.

The last pointed questions go to black Americans. If you have cultivated in your children a respect and appreciation for education as an 'opportunity', do you think they will need any special consideration? Does indefinitely continuing the policy of affirmative action not ultimately go against the basic value of equality of opportunity?

For several generations young American men and women of all races have fought side-by-side in a number of wars to defend American values. Can't we all reach the same point here at home? Shouldn't we be able to stand for these values even if it means taking a stand against some of our own ethnic group? Then we as individuals will know that we are truly *American*, and not at all racist. The more we are truly American, in values not in ethnicity, the stronger and more just America will be.

And the stronger and more just we are in the world, the better our chances of cultivating a stable, secure, and potentially steadily improving world.

CHAPTER 8.

A BALANCED BUDGET

The need to begin thinking beyond what we want now has already been mentioned, and that notion is most applicable right in the middle of a discussion of taxes and spending, of entitlements and reasonable expectations, and of who benefits and how from our collective purse. In the <u>very</u> near future we must move from discussing these issues to doing something about them. Economists much more familiar with the details than I have been stressing that the long-term economic health of our nation depends on getting our financial house in order. The question I will look at is "How?"

Many have no-doubt noted the irony of President Bush calling for increased "volunteerism" in constructive community activities while also calling for larger tax cuts for the very richest segment of our society. Sometimes the degree to which the far right has succeeded in duping so many of us amazes me.

I don't know many truly wealthy folks, but I do remember one of them complaining off-handedly that he pays more than his share of taxes, and all the while doesn't benefit from <u>any</u> government program. My reply was direct: "You benefit from the **# 1** government program... providing for and ensuring societal stability. If not for the stability around you, you couldn't have accumulated your wealth. And if not for continued stability around you, you won't be able to maintain your wealth." After a pause he nodded, but went on to note the degree of waste that happens in the government's distribution of other benefits. The "average" wealthy citizen isn't duped so much as unrecognizing of the reality of their benefits.

The average hard-working middle class citizen bought into the low-tax mantra of the right because the tax-and-spend mentality of the left had gone too far. That's legitimate. We got duped though into buying the idea that, no matter what societal service is sacrificed, lower is always better when it comes to taxes. Further, we got duped into the idea that whatever someone can earn in a free market economy, they "deserve" it. Be patient now, I'm not a commie, and I will explain.

I cannot and will not argue that they "**don't** deserve" what they get any more than someone can argue that they "**do** deserve" what they get. I believe in the free market economy, and if professional athletes, corporate

CEOs, high-powered attorneys, movie stars, etc. happen to be able to command a lot in our system, so be it. It is simply what they **can** get, and "deserving" it isn't for us to question **or** to concede. For us to bow like humble lambs and say that they shouldn't pay more is being duped.

#21. Having a higher tax rate, a progressive and substantially higher one, for the extremely wealthy isn't confiscatory or punitive… it simply has them pay disproportionately into supporting the free enterprise system from which they benefit disproportionately.

Despite what some may be muttering at this point, I am not a tax-and-spend liberal. I know very well that socialism, carried to its extreme, will suffocate itself like a beached blue whale. I am pointing out though that capitalism, carried to its extreme, will dismember nearly all of its participants like a bunch of chomping beetles enclosed in too small a container. Yes, on one hand we need our true fiscal conservatives acting as our constant watch-dogs against government waste (and corruption!); but on the other hand we must recognize that we need to continue to tweek capitalism to bring out the broad best in our society. Despite elitist mantra that a lower tax rate for the wealthy is good for the economy, there is nothing good about increasing deficits.

There are people from building contractors to custodians to small business owners who have for a good while voted republican, who are now questioning the party line. They have pride in their hard work, and don't like the idea of the lazy mooching off of their taxes, and that has made them conservatives. But they are seeing the excesses of the elite, of the very wealthy, and they are questioning their allegiance. The tide has begun to shift.

It doesn't have to be at one extreme or the other. Picture the numbers 1 through 10 spread in front of you, left to right. At 1 we have tree huggers… folks who have no respect for the value of jobs in the economy, who think of any little creature as of equal value to a human life. At 10 we have corporate heavy lifters… folks whose bottom line is "a buck now," who have no respect for tomorrow and what it brings to all of our descendants.

It might be constructive to take a moment and reflect on which end of that spectrum 1-10 has lately been in power the most, and whether or not we want it to stay that way. The extremes don't have to win if we in the middle stand up and speak up.

We need to struggle with and resolve a number of specifics along these lines. The President was right to bring our attention to the non-sustainability of the social security program as it now exists… another instance of him showing some foresight. The type of solution he proposed though has been rejected at least in part because so many people recognize that he hasn't even seriously considered other partial solutions that are reasonable. Why should social security deductions stop on incomes over any certain point? The increased SS intake if that were changed would make a substantial difference.

Some are again going to whine about that being confiscatory, but again, it simply helps look out for the stability of the broader society by having those who have benefited disproportionately from the free market system support disproportionately that same system. It doesn't argue with the fact that they can and have benefited.

22. We have already made other adjustments that affect the average and poor… full SS benefits are available only at increasing ages, as it should be. If a system that was designed to look out for the broader good can make adjustments that affect the masses, surely it can make adjustments that affect the privileged.

23. The need for significant adjustments to reality in programs like Medicaid and Medicare is pressing too. In these cases it may be that we baby-boomers need to just suck it up and realize that not everything we wish for can be.

Several paragraphs back I referred to the under-standable reaction of hard-working members of our society to the excesses of the tax-and-spend left… to not liking being abused by the lazy. That's real. There are two questions though, that are sometimes not analyzed. 1. Are there any members of our society who do need and deserve our support? And 2. Can you completely eliminate abuse from any large bureaucracy?

If we have the guts and callous to answer the first with "No," then we can move on without the second. We could have an official policy of social Darwinism. If you're fit, you survive; if not, tough. If however, our answer to the first is "Yes," then we must struggle with the second.

Anyone who runs a small business with say six employees can first-handedly ensure that they are not wasteful and inefficient. But as driven and competitive as Bill Gates and most of his Microsoft employees are, he still can't ensure complete efficiency throughout a relatively large bureaucracy. This is not to say that we should sigh and accept all manner of governmental inefficiency. No! In fact we owe a debt of gratitude to the real fiscal conservatives who have battled government waste. But it is to say that the inevitable existence of some level of waste is not a good excuse for wielding a battle axe at whole programs that do address some real needs and issues of the broader good.

It will be interesting to watch the far right and see if they ultimately develop a split between the extreme fiscal conservatives (who include some avowed Christians) whose politics are basically social Darwinism, and the more moderate (which includes other Christians who recognize degrees of socialism in scripture... Acts 4 and James for starters).

Having brought up the issues of government waste and real fiscal conservatives I can't resist raising one more challenge to mid-Americans. On many pork barrel spending attachments, voters in 49 states recognize the abuse that is going on; but voters in the one state involved go along with the ludicrous because it benefits them. It may be asking a lot, it may even border on the unrealistic, but if we all asked ourselves if the proposed project is good for more than "us," and if we were then willing to speak up in protest to our own representatives and senators, and to vote out corruption and cronyism, we might eliminate a lot of waste on our own.

BEYOND A BALANCED BUDGET... A BALANCED APPROACH TO GOVERNANCE AND LIFE

In wrapping up this attempt to help us look toward the long-term over the immediate, toward the good of society over "me," it may be worthwhile to review at least one real case in the battle over government's role. I lived in southern California in the late 80s. We often couldn't see not only the San Bernardino Mountains thirty miles away, but we couldn't even see the hills only two miles in the other direction. Now you can enjoy both views; the air is qualitatively and quantitatively very different. It is very unlikely that without government regulation that change would have happened.

I now live in a small town in southern Oregon. Our air used to be polluted, not by un-numbered vehicles but by unregulated wood burning. The same positive change in air quality has been accomplished here too, for the same reason. But an irony from the other side has shown its head here recently. Our county is big by almost any standard, and our town of still slightly less than 50,000 including the suburbs is a small drop of urban life in a spacious rural landscape. Our landfill site was filling up, and a decision had to be made on what to do next.

Discussions of trucking our wastes over mountain passes or shipping it by rail to distant sites seemed to be all we heard or read. The inefficiency of these being obvious to me, I called to ask why in such an area of open spaces we couldn't just get a new and relatively local landfill site. The guy almost laughed. His reply was something like, "The number of hoops we'd have to jump through, the number of <u>years</u> it would take to get a new landfill site approved, make it basically undoable."

How ironic. Laws intended to help us safe-guard our environment, the same general set of laws that helped us clean up our air, are now making us do the least efficient and sensible thing with our solid waste.

The line between good government and big government isn't always obvious and is easily crossed. The left tends to want tons of government; the right tends to want no government except an army. To these two extreme segments who have unthinking loyalty to a party line, add a here-to-fore too silent middle, and a media which likes to create neat categories (red vs. blue etc.) where reality shows complexities involving single-digit differences, and you have a recipe for governance from the extremes. It is time that **We** changed that.

#24. It is up to all of us to make sure that government is and does what is right.

The author can be contacted by visiting

simpletruths.biz

www.ingramcontent.com/pod-product-compliance
Lightning Source LLC
Chambersburg PA
CBHW020247290526
45784CB00003B/1129